THE FIRST
AMENDMENT
IN A FREE SOCIETY

edited by JONATHAN BARTLETT

THE REFERENCE SHELF
Volume 50 Number 6

THE H. W. WILSON COMPANY
New York 1979

THE REFERENCE SHELF

The books in this series contain reprints of articles, excerpts from books, and addresses on current issues and social trends in the United States and other countries. There are six separately bound numbers in each volume, all of which are generally published in the same calendar year. One number is a collection of recent speeches; each of the others is devoted to a single subject and gives background information and discussion from various points of view, concluding with a comprehensive bibliography. Books in the series may be purchased individually or on subscription.

342.73
Fir

Library of Congress Cataloging in Publication Data

Main entry under title:

The First Amendment in a Free Society.

(The Reference shelf ; v. 50, no. 6)
Bibliography: p.
1. Liberty of the press—United States   —Addresses,
essays, lectures. 2. Obscenity (law)—United States
—Addresses, essays, lectures. 3. Assembly (right of)
—Illinois—Skokie   —Addresses, essays, lectures.
4. Religious liberty—United States   —Addresses,
essays, lectures. I. Bartlett, Jonathan, 1931. II.
Series.
KF4770.A75F57   342.73085   78-27806
ISBN 0-8242-0627-4

International Standard Book Number 0–8242–0627–4
PRINTED IN THE UNITED STATES OF AMERICA

PREFACE

Congress shall make no law respecting an establishment of religion, or prohibiting the free exercise thereof; or abridging the freedom of speech, or of the press; or the right of the people peaceably to assemble, and to petition the government for a redress of grievances.

So states the First Amendment to the Constitution of the United States, the first of ten amendments known collectively as the Bill of Rights. Other amendments included in the Bill of Rights refer to such guaranties as the right to bear arms, the regulating of the government's right of search and seizure, the right to a fair trial. The fact that matters like speech, press, religion, and assembly are the subjects of the very First Amendment may well reflect the priorities of Thomas Jefferson, expressed in a letter to James Madison, strongly urging the inclusion of a bill of rights, written in December 1787, after Jefferson had read the proposed Constitution. In his letter, Jefferson seemed especially concerned with the question of religion, although speech and the press were also stressed, and Madison seems to have followed the wishes of his Virginia colleague closely, although he himself had been at best lukewarm to the concept. But Jefferson's persuasion, coupled with the realization that so crucial a state as Massachusetts would probably not ratify the Constitution without the promise of a Bill of Rights, helped carry the day. Twelve amendments (later pared to ten) were drafted, mostly by Madison himself, and after approval by the Congress and ratification by the states, became part of the Constitution in 1791.

The Bill of Rights was not adopted without challenging debate. Those of the Federalist persuasion, looking for a strong central government, saw no need to prohibit Congress from regulating any behavior that the Constitution did not give it the power to regulate anyway. The real substance of

3

this position was conveyed by Alexander Hamilton in Number 84 of the Federalist Papers, a series of articles arguing for the ratification of the Constitution and written chiefly by Hamilton, Madison, and John Jay.

I go further, and affirm that bills of right, in the sense and to the extent in which they are contended for, are not only unnecessary in the proposed Constitution, but would even be dangerous. They would contain various exceptions to powers not granted; and, on this very account, would afford a colorable pretext to claim more than were granted. For why declare that things shall not be done which there is no power to do? Why, for instance, should it be said that the liberty of the press shall not be restrained, when no power is given by which restrictions may be imposed? I will not contend that such a provision would confer a regulating power, but it is evident that it would furnish, to men disposed to usurp, a plausible pretence for claiming that power.

In opposition to the Federalists were Anti-Federalists, who seemed to be of two minds, united only in their desire to see the states hold power as against the central government. The more moderate among them insisted upon adding a bill of rights to temper any autocratic tendencies a central government might show, whereas the radicals seemed to want to scotch the Constitution entirely, or at least reconvene a convention to rewrite it to conform more closely to the Articles of Confederation that had so dismally failed—and thereby prompted the writing of the Constitution itself.

It would seem, on historical evidence, that Jefferson and the moderate Anti-Federalists, in their insistence on a Bill of Rights, were more far-seeing than Hamilton and the more rigid of the Federalists. Indeed, despite the straightforward language and obvious intent of the First Amendment, there have been from time to time in the nation's history serious setbacks to the freedoms it was designed to preserve. Perhaps the first was the Sedition Act of 1798, passed at a time when President John Adams' Federalist government not only feared the radical views associated with revolutionary France, but also wished to silence political opposition at home. The law made it illegal to publish false or malicious writings about the government or to incite opposition to the congress or the president. A number of people were fined or jailed, including twenty-four editors of pro-Republican newspapers. One man, Republican Congressman Matthew Lyon, was jailed for four months and fined $1,000 simply for having written a letter, published in a Vermont newspaper, that criticized the government for its "ridiculous pomp, foolish adulation, and selfish avarice." Luckily, the Sedition Act lapsed in 1800 and Jefferson, by then President, did not renew it.

In another setback a number of people were convicted under the Sedition Law of 1918, which was designed to punish those who spoke or wrote in a way that might be deemed to interfere with the war effort or cause contempt for the government. The Supreme Court sustained the convictions in all six cases it considered, but in one, *Abrams v. United States* (1919) Justice Holmes, who with Brandeis dissented from the Court's decision, wrote these words: ". . . the ultimate good desired is better reached by free trade in ideas . . . the best test of truth is the power of the thought to get itself accepted in the competition of the market."

The articles in this compilation discuss a number of recent cases that illustrate, collectively, just how difficult it is to agree on what the First Amendment protects and what it does not. The matter is complicated by the fact the First Amendment is often invoked to protect kinds of activity for which many—perhaps even most—people in this country have a strong distaste. The distribution of obscene material is one such activity, and it is the subject of the articles in Chapter 1. Is pornography an element of free speech? As you will see, the answer to that thorny question depends in part on whose definition of obscenity is being applied.

Chapter 2 deals briefly with freedom of religion, which is by now a pretty well settled matter in this country—perhaps more so than any other right protected under the First Amendment. Still, there have been recent cases involving the forcible "deprogramming" of converts to certain religious cults in which violations of Constitutional rights may be involved. Chapter 2 also covers several cases on freedom of the press, the most widely reported area of First Amendment concern.

Chapter 3 pursues the matter of freedom of the press by focusing on a controversial and possibly historic case: that of the New York *Times* reporter Myron Abba Farber, who went to jail for refusing to turn over to a court in a first-degree murder trial his notes made during the case's original investigation.

Chapter 4, on the right of assembly, runs true to controversial form by presenting articles on the bitter argument in Illinois over whether American Nazis could hold a parade on the Fourth of July in the heavily Jewish city of Skokie.

The First Amendment has always shielded—and doubtless will continue to do so—a wide (and often unpopular) range of activities, writings, and beliefs. How wide, how unpopular? It is hoped that this compilation will give the reader not answers, but some feeling for the issues and debates—all of them of concern to our society—aroused by the questions.

The Editor particularly wishes to thank the authors and publishers who have granted permission to reprint the materials that make up this compilation. And in closing, he especially wishes to thank the staff of the New York City Public Library system, who have made courtesy and helpfulness a way of life and created a haven for any researcher.

CONTENTS

I. OBSCENITY—WHAT'S IN A WORD?

EDITOR'S INTRODUCTION

The question of what constitutes "proper" language and what is "indelicate" (or worse) has vexed society probably since society began. In England following the Norman conquest of 1066, "gentlefolk" spoke Norman French, leaving Anglo-Saxon to swineherds and similar rabble. Even today when we dine we serve beef (from the French *boeuf*) or veal (from the French *veau*) whereas our farmers and cowboys— those who *work* with the animals—occupy themselves with bulls, cows, and calfs (calf derived from Anglo-Saxon). Other Anglo-Saxonisms will surely spring readily to mind. One question that often arises is whether certain words are in and of themselves obscene. If so, can their publication or other dissemination be prohibited by law? In other words, should a writer be able to put down in his work words that are considered "obscene," and does the First Amendment's guarantee of free speech permit him to do so? Until 1935, the answer was that the writer could not. In that year, Random House, a New York publishing firm, determined to find out if the postal authorities had the constitutional authority to ban the importation—as they were doing—of James Joyce's even-then critically acclaimed *Ulysses*. In an historic decision, Judge John M. Woolsey of the United States District Court lifted the ban and proclaimed it legal to import and distribute the book in the United States, basing his argument on the First Amendment. Later such books as *Lady Chatterley's Lover* and *Fanny Hill* worked their ways through the courts and gained, if not respectability, at least legal acceptance. The printed word seems now to be relatively immune to prosecution, and obscenity issues are focused more upon broadcasting and graphic expression—illustrations and films, especially. Two First Amendment issues remain: the definition of what is obscene and whether, if something is obscene, it should or even can be suppressed.

In current rulings on convictions under state obscenity statutes, the Supreme Court relies on its 1973 *Miller v. California* decision which requires that the work in question, taken as a whole, must appeal to prurient interest as determined by *applying contemporary community standards* and that the work, taken as a whole, lacks serious literary, artistic, political, or scientific value.

The first article, by Peter Michelson in the *Nation*, illustrates the difficulty of making the *Miller v. California* guidelines into workable—i.e., enforceable—law on the local level. The next two articles, the first from *Newsweek* by Richard Boeth with Elaine Sciolino and the second, from *National Review*, discuss, from different vantage points, the Kansas case against Al Goldstein and James Buckley on twelve counts of obscenity.

The fourth article "The Filthy Words Decision," unsigned in *America*, gives the details of a recent Supreme Court decision on broadcast material that the Court ruled not obscene but "patently offensive."

M. J. Sobran, senior editor of *National Review*, argues strongly that since freedom of speech is not absolute it should not be expected to protect obscenity any more than it protects libelous material and that as a society, we must come up with a definition, "a systematic explication of the idea of obscenity with reference to the related ideas of privacy, sexual morality and symbolism, and the authority of social convention."

Finally, in a view very different from that of Mr. Sobran, Charles Rembar, a lawyer who has specialized in First Amendment cases (*Lady Chatterley's Lover, Fanny Hill*), suggests that we must discard the present anachronistic concept of obscenity in order to deal with so-called objectionable material or behavior on legal grounds that do not dilute the guaranties of the First Amendment.

THE WAY THE WIND BLOWS [1]

Boulder, Colorado, where winds frequently whip out of the Rockies at speeds up to 100 miles per hour, is a town where one can also get a feel for which way the nation's cultural winds blow. It may not be the heart of the heart of the country, but it does seem to provide an index of the fluctuations of liberalism and conservatism in American life. Its most recent instance is the city's prosecution of a pornography case that, in terms of establishing legal criteria for obscenity, seems to have national implications.

Around the corner from Boulder High School a fast-food shop went out of business last summer and an adult bookstore called The News Stand moved in; it features the usual pornographic books, magazines and arcade of films. The move was geographically inept. In September, just after school opened, a group of parents complained to the District Attorney's office of the store's proximity to the high school. Meanwhile, Boulder's other and older smut shop, ironically located across the street from the District Attorney's office, elicited no complaints.

For a variety of reasons—chiefly, perhaps, their lack of success in court, due to broad and ambiguous state statutes—district attorneys across the country are unenthusiastic about pornography litigation. So as public attention focused on the Boulder matter, District Attorney Alex Hunter "staked out" The News Stand, and was able to report that no "undesirable characters" had been observed hanging around, and that, furthermore, when a 17-year-old "agent" was sent to make a purchase, the store had refused, as per its posted policy on minors, to admit or serve him. Hunter also announced that he was waiting for a Denver case to determine the constitutionality of the state's new obscenity statute. He obviously hoped by these means to settle the dust, but the

[1] From article entitled "Obscenity and the Law: the Way the Wind Blows," by Peter Michelson, member of Department of English, University of Colorado, and author of The Aesthetics of Pornography. The Nation. 226:105–8. F. 4, '78. Reprinted by permission of The Nation Associates.

Citizens Action Committee continued its agitation until, when finally the school board requested some action, Hunter's hand was forced.

He appointed Jack Kerner, like himself young and liberal, to handle the case, and they filed a civil rather than criminal action against The News Stand. Specifically, they charged that five fairly typical hard-core magazines violated the Colorado statute. The statute is a tortuous product of the Supreme Court's landmark *Miller v. California* decision of 1973. Justice Burger's majority opinion in *Miller* revealed the distasteful morality play that the obscenity business had become for the Supreme Court. Citing Justice Brennan, he notes, "that the examination of contested materials 'is hardly a source of edification to members of this Court.' " And with the dissenting voices of Justices Black and Douglas obviously haunting him, he wants once and for all to entomb the perturbed spirit of the "absolutist" view of First Amendment rights: "In this belief, however," he says, "Mr. Justice Douglas now stands alone." Then he goes on to say with relief that, "today, for the first time since *Roth* was decided in 1957, a majority of this Court has agreed on concrete guidelines to isolate 'hard-core' pornography from expression protected by the First Amendment. Now we may abandon . . . casual practice . . . and attempt to provide positive guidance to the federal and state courts alike."

But if the Justices were relieved, state legislatures still had a job of work to do, translating the guidelines of the *Miller* opinion into workable law. With consistent help from Colorado district attorneys—an El Paso County D.A. testified plaintively, "If the people of Colorado want obscenity laws enforced, give us the tools"—the Colorado legislature, after three years of hearings and false starts, finally got its act together this past July. It follows the Burger Court majority in reaffirming, though not without some contradiction, "that obscene material is not protected by the First Amendment," in holding that "contemporary community standards" of prurience are "statewide" rather than "national," in attempting to specify what representations of sex acts are "patently offensive" and thus liable to court action, and in releasing prosecutors from the obligation to prove that obscene material is "*utterly*" without redeeming social value." (The Colorado statute's phrasing is, "Taken as a whole, lacks serious literary, artistic, political, or scientific value.")

From the "absolutist" standpoint it is as bad a statute as one might expect. From the middle-of-the-road perspective of a Justice Brennan one can say that it does make an effort to accommodate obscenity of a "serious" social sort. However, just as the Burger opinion blithely passes over clinkers if not outright contradictions (Brennan, for example, had maintained "that no formulation of this Court, the Congress, or the States can adequately distinguish obscene material unprotected by the First Amendment from protected expression"), so the Colorado statute harbors "flaws" (e.g., it makes lending or receiving obscene materials a culpable offense, but the written word is altogether exempted from its jurisdiction) that may well send the whole thing back to committee again. Be that as it may, this was the statute on which The News Stand was prosecuted, and successfully prosecuted, in Boulder. It was understood from the outset that the loser would appeal to the Colorado Supreme Court. In fact Arthur Schwartz, defense attorney not only for The News Stand but in a gaggle of obscenity cases across the country, forced the constitutional issue at the local level by stipulating that his client's material was indeed obscene according to the statute, but that the statute was unconstitutionally broad and vague in its injunctions. He raised the ante, he said, because he had "a feeling" the Boulder court would rule against him, so he decided to save his client (and Boulder County) considerable expense by going directly to an appeal.

Several cases throughout Colorado, including Denver, are awaiting the outcome of this appeal. And prosecutor Kerner thinks that, because the Colorado law not only was modeled on the California one affirmed in *Miller* but is even more specific in designating liable obscenity, cases in other states are also awaiting the Colorado judgment; moreover, that the Colorado statute will serve as a model for other state legislatures. Though he himself gives a low priority to prosecuting obscenity, he thinks the statute workable from a D.A.'s point of view and fair to porn dealers in that it clearly informs them what the law allows. That, if upheld, it may well put them out of business is another matter. Kerner thinks that the prevailing winds of obscenity litigation are what they seem—conservative. So he echoes the sentiments of his El Paso County colleague: if the people of Colorado want obscenity laws enforced, their D.A.s now have a useful tool. But Schwartz challenges that view right down the line.

For a Denver attorney he covers a lot of ground, being involved with obscenity cases in Ogden, Seattle, Kansas City, New York, North Carolina and Florida. So he draws on trial experience from a variety of contemporary communities. While he acknowledges a conservative shift from the Warren to the Burger Court, he sees that movement in a more subtle sociological context than D.A.s can by and large afford to contemplate. The district attorneys are in a political bind. Though, as did Hunter in Boulder, they hear vociferously from censorship proponents, they know that many of their constituents support a laissez-faire policy toward obscenity, even when they do not bother to say so. Political constituencies vary, but Schwartz thinks the current estimate of rising conservatism is overrated. He finds that the "average juror is unwilling to follow the Court" in obscenity adjudication and "will go to any length to find redeeming value" in pornographic material. He cites not only his trial experience to support this view but electoral politics as well. He notes, for instance, that in Ogden a group of City Council members who supported aggressive prosecution of obscenity were defeated in a recent election. And in Seattle a referendum, Initiative 335, even though worded so ambiguously as to suggest falsely that it applied only to "kiddie porn," passed by the narrow margin of 460,000 to 400,000 votes. Moreover, he says, even Billy Graham came out in support of an anti-Initiative group called Life, on the ground that the inclination toward censorship should be curbed.

So Schwartz doubts that the people of Colorado or any-where else really want obscenity laws enforced with the fervor D.A.s may suppose. Not, he alds, that the "average juror" has a passionate commitment to First Amendment rights but he does have common sense. Primarily, Schwartz thinks, jurors are quite aware that there are more important things on which to spend ever thinning tax resources (many D.A.s, including Kerner, hold that opinion).

Beyond that, he detects a disinclination to have the law butt in where it's not needed; after all, he observes, jurors know that "nobody *has* to buy porn, and people's personal tastes are their own." It follows, then, that Schwartz prefers to defend his clients before a jury. Judges, in a bind similar to that of D.A.s, are often loath to be identified publicly with any tolerance for obscenity. And, the law being their profession, they are perhaps more inclined than the average citizen to give its rationale and history precedence over com-mon sense. If Justice Burger equates obscenity with heroin and says, "civilized people do not allow unregulated access" to either, then Judge X of Yoknapatawpha County may very well agree, even though he has not personally ever thought himself in danger of addiction to either drug. Schwartz recognizes that there are a few "courageous judges" who will throw bad laws back in the teeth of state legislators. He cites Judge Manos of the US District Court in Ohio as a case in point. But he has a historical hypothesis that he thinks explains the current situation. The liberal Warren Court, he thinks, assumed a role of leadership and ventured into "progressive" constitutional interpretations that the times required. The conservative Burger Court, on the other hand, wants to hold the line and is therefore more restrictive and less responsive to social dynamics. The consequence, so far as obscenity litigation is concerned, is that the people are now leading the Court rather than the other way around.

So far as *Miller* goes, Schwartz sees a couple of ironies. Even though it encourages exercise of broad discretionary powers by local D.A.s and courts, he claims to be having more success than before in winning cases at the trial level. For *Miller* in effect invalidated most state obscenity statutes because of their ambiguity. Enterprising distributors of pornography quickly noticed what was happening and began to disseminate their products both more widely and more discreetly. The "boarding house reach" of business is quicker by far than the arm of law. That, of course, is why the Boulder News Stand case is important. It is not simply a test of the Colorado statute but also an index of whether *Miller*'s legislative influence can keep pace not only with the "average juror" and the porn industry but with itself as well. That is, it remains to be seen nationally whether the *Miller* guidelines do in fact sufficiently instruct state legislators so that they can provide D.A.s with a genuinely workable tool, one that will in practice stand up to constitutional requirements.

Schwartz, who credits the Colorado Supreme Court with being "pretty good" on First Amendment matters, thinks there is "no question" but that it will reverse the Boulder court's decision. Unlike Kerner, he thinks the Colorado statute broader and more vague than the California law on which it was modeled. Further, in an obvious effort not to encroach in any way on literature, it exempts "the printed or written word." Schwartz construes that to violate equal protection rights, but Boulder Judge Richard Dana's decision maintains that the printed word is not exempt if it is published together with pictures. In fact, the Colorado statute is more precise than its California counterpart in designating what sexual conduct it is impermissible to represent, but it does unequivocally exempt the printed or written word, as the California statute does not. Judge Dana's logic is clear enough, that it must be possible to censor an illegal picture in company with a legal text, but his ruling simultaneously confirms the law in regard to pictures while in effect it violates the law in regard to words. The statute itself does not clarify the legal status of a publication so divided. Nor is this confusion resolved by the statute's oft-repeated phrase regarding material which, "taken as a whole, lacks

serious literary, artistic, political, or scientific value." It puts
the matter right back into the interpretive bog from which
the statute was trying to remove it, this time weighing the
redeemable word against the irredeemable picture. And on
such particulars does the law sometimes turn. So this may
be the clinker that justifies Schwartz's optimism.

Schwartz is prepared to take The News Stand case to the
US Supreme Court if the Colorado court fails him. But if
anything the current US Court, without Douglas, is more
conservative than it was in 1973. As one reads through the
Miller opinion and sees its profound influence on the Colorado statute one has unmistakably to feel that obscenity laws
are becoming, if not better, at least sharper. And one marvels
at the years judges and legislators have spent plugging up
loopholes only to have new ones open behind them. Clearly
these servants of the people are determined to serve and protect. But what if, as Schwartz and his colleagues argue and
many a D.A. will confirm in private, the people less and less
feel a need for protection against obscenity? What if the
people think obscenity an insufficiently serious problem to
justify those years at public expense? At the moment one
cannot say with confidence that in fact the people do so
think, but there is evidence to suggest evolution in that direction. In *Miller* Justice Burger observes that, "This may
not be an easy road, free from difficulty. But no amount of
'fatigue' should lead us to adopt a convenient 'institutional'
rationale . . . because it will lighten our burdens." The
"institution" to which he refers with such uneasiness is the
Constitution. And his notion of a "civilized people's" burden is tiresome whichever way you see it. If The News Stand
decision is reversed, does the Colorado legislature start over,
or proceed one patch at a time? If it is upheld the consequences seem even more thankless. Five nondescript smut
magazines that were probably out of print the moment they
were published will be found illegal in the state of Colorado.
To extend the case any further than that will take more

litigation—more time, more money. And The News Stand itself? A quiet little place that doesn't admit minors and has no hangers-on at all, let alone evil ones.

Obscenity has become a South Sea Bubble, generating itself on Manichean phantasmagoria of good and evil locked in battle. This is not to say that the voices calling for protection from smut *should* be ignored; they probably do represent that slim majority suggested by the Seattle referendum results. But it is to suggest that the legislative, judicial and police energy spent on obscenity is an "expense of spirit in a waste of shame." The very efforts of the Colorado legislature to exempt the printed word from censorship are an ironic example of obscenity winds blowing at crosspurposes. It is a piece of "progressive" legislation without precedent in either *Miller* or *Roth*. And it in fact refutes the philosophy that inspired it. For its cultural implication is that the word, even the most blatantly obscene word, *does* have First Amendment protection. Moreover the statute exempts "persons employed by a university, college, or library." Why are such persons, whether janitors or professors, more privileged or less corruptible than anybody else?

Apart from the legal considerations that account for such wording, the implication of these exemptions is a lefthanded and grudging acknowledgment that "Congress shall make no law . . . abridging freedom of speech or of the press." In short, we are constantly reminded that all laws abridging these freedoms, however persuasively their need is argued (and it is not far from the point that legislatures are not obliged to demonstrate a *need*), are always second best. Why else is it that, according to the statute, D.A.s "may institute" action against obscenity rather than that they *must*? Even in this most ingenious devising of obscenity law our legislators have left us a way out. Each time around obscenity legislation proves to be a house divided against itself. Whichever way the wind blows from the Colorado or the United States Supreme Court, the time cannot be many years off when the sheer windiness of the whole enterprise will collapse the house inward upon itself.

OBSCENITY: WHO'S TO SAY? [2]

Late in 1973, on orders from the Postmaster's office in Washington, postal officials in the Kansas towns of Lawrence, Salina, Hutchinson and Pratt were given money orders and told to purchase, under assumed names, four mail subscriptions to two New York-based tabloids called *Screw* and *Smut*. When their copies began arriving in Kansas, the postal officials—still following Federal instructions—logged their appearance and mailed them back to New York in their unopened brown envelopes. These maneuvers finally came to a head last week as the owner of the two tabloids, Al Goldstein, and his former partner, James Buckley, sat in a Federal district courtroom in Kansas City, Kansas, to face twelve counts of obscenity—in accordance with the US Supreme Court's Miller decision of 1973 that defines obscenity in terms of local community standards.

By all standards, the Buckley-Goldstein case is a landmark in the ongoing and apparently unavailing effort to find a neat and workable legal formula for dealing with obscenity. For the prosecution, the case is the furthest extension of the Miller decision so far attempted at a Federal level. Previously, communities had moved against allegedly obscene materials only when their sensibilities were publicly flouted—in newsstand displays, movie theaters or, in the case of *Hustler* magazine, by local publication. In Kansas, none of these criteria applies. *Screw*, a nine-year-old tabloid with a national circulation of 130,000, had only ten brown-wrapper subscribers in all of Kansas and *Smut* only one—aside from the postal inspectors—and neither was sold on any newsstand in the state. What is so unusual is that the Federal government is seeking to obtain conviction on the abstract ground that the "standards" of a community were offended, even if no people were.

[2] Article by Richard Boeth and Elaine Sciolino. *Newsweek*. 90:53. N. 7, '77.

"The Net Effect"

To civil libertarians and many constitutional scholars, the Kansas case represents a major threat to all publications with national distribution—as well as a demonstration of the unworkability of the Miller formula. "If a publisher wants to play it safe, he has to attempt to figure out what is the most restrictive, conservative notion of obscenity in the country and not publish anything that violates that standard," says Geoffrey Stone, associate professor of law at the University of Chicago. "The net effect is that the rights of citizens in every other location are impaired."

Some legal experts also believe that Goldstein and Buckley were the victims of "geographical" entrapment by postal officials eager to bring the case in the least hospitable venue. "It's a bloody outrage," says Harvard Law School's Alan Dershowitz. "You trick Goldstein into a jurisdiction when he's not selling on the newsstands or committing a crime there. It represents one of the most dangerous precedents in the area of free speech I have ever experienced." Says assistant US attorney Ben Burgess, who heads the prosecution: "People like Al Goldstein act at their own risk when they send their publications out in the country."

Defense counsel Herald Price Fahringer, a First Amendment specialist from Buffalo, says that he intends to argue the case on still a third ground—"that the real issue is whether or not adults should be able to read and see what they please." Some legal experts question whether this will play, since it's the publishers, not the readers of *Screw* and *Smut*, who are on trial. Though it may seem odd to hold the purveyor guilty and not the user as well, the distinction is common enough in law—in the prosecution of prostitution, for instance, and many marijuana cases.

"Bad Boy?"

What no one denies is that *Screw* and *Smut* are as scuzzy, smarmy and squamous as any publications ever printed. Even Al Goldstein—a rotund 41-year-old who likens himself to a "bad boy who writes f--- on the walls of his parents' bathroom"—acknowledges that *Screw* is "tasteless and disgusting," though he insists that "it's not obscene." Whatever the word, the tabloids present tactical problems for the defense. At the first Buckley-Goldstein trial in Wichita last year—which was declared a mistrial—defense lawyers did little to forewarn the jurors, and one woman juror reportedly burst into tears when she viewed the evidence. This time, Fahringer has given the jurors—seven women and five men—sneak previews "of what they would see—oral sex, intercourse, bestiality."

The prosecution is also preparing a little more carefully. At the first trial, prosecutor Larry Schauf, now in corporate practice, characterized Goldstein as "the mayor of 42nd Street" and repeatedly accused him of trying to introduce degeneracy and indecency into Kansas. Since the law under the Miller decision does not take into account social effects —only whether the material is obscene or not—and since 42nd Street was not on trial anyway, US District Judge Frank G. Theis finally declared a mistrial after several warnings.

Though defense lawyers claim to be happier with the Kansas City venue than they were with Wichita, Goldstein is pessimistic. "There's no doubt I'll get jail," he said last week. "It's alien territory here." Fahringer agrees. "Kansas is a dry state with a history of anti-pornography crusades." Co-defendant Buckley, a slight, clean-cut 33-year-old who lives with his wife in an eighteen-room country mansion he bought from Norman Mailer, is almost as gloomy. "We were under indictment a hundred times," he reflects. "This one seemed like such a setup that I never took it seriously."

"Censor"

If Goldstein and Buckley lose, the case will almost certainly be appealed on constitutional grounds to test whether the Miller formula is tenable. "Any community can act as the censor of any other community—that's small-town censorship," says Dershowitz. "*Screw* is a despicable magazine, but

that's what the First Amendment was designed to protect."
At the end of the road, it may be that the US Supreme Court
—which hoped with the Miller decision to wash its hands of
obscenity cases—will have to start grappling with the tricky
issue all over again.

FIRST AMENDMENT PIXILLATION [3]

Freedom of the press is in mortal peril again, this time
out in Kansas, where pseudonymous postal officials tricked
New York pornographer Al Goldstein into mailing them
his brainchildren, *Screw* and *Smut*. Civil libertarians are
swarming to the defense of Goldstein and his former partner, one James Buckley . . . who are now on trial on federal
charges of mailing obscene materials. "*Screw* is a despicable
publication," says Harvard's Alan Dershowitz, "but that's
what the First Amendment was designed to protect." False.
That's what the First Amendment is currently *used* to protect, but . . . well, class, let's have a short review.

Until very recently nobody suggested that the First
Amendment had been intended to protect obscenity. Or
that it should be *stretched* to protect it. As for the first point,
the record is clear: obscenity, like incitement to riot, has
traditionally been illegal. And the intentions of the Framers
are limned with shocking clarity in Leonard Levy's *Legacy
of Suppression*. Judge Wolsey's [sic] famous ruling in
Ulysses, let it be recalled, denied that *Ulysses* was obscene
simply as a matter of fact (more emetic than aphrodisiac, he
sniffed), without faintly suggesting that nothing was obscene,
or that the law should not take cognizance of—and punish—
obscene publications. As a matter of fact, the US struggled
along for almost two centuries uninundated by the likes of
Screw, and is it suggested that during those years American
thought was stultified? As for the contention that the First
Amendment should be stretched, well, that is incompatible
with the principle of the rule of law. Let those who want it

    [3] Unsigned article. *National Review*. 29:1349–50. N. 25, '77. Reprinted by
permission of *National Review*, 150 E. 35th St., New York, NY 10016.

changed get another Amendment. Of course they can't: their whole case depends heavily on forging a phony constitutional pedigree for their libertarianism, and only deludes people because they have succeeded in intimating that the Constitution has already committed us, whether we like it or not, to . . . *Screw*.

Yet here is Geoffrey Stone of the University of Chicago: "If a publisher wants to play it safe, he has to attempt to figure out what is the most restrictive, conservative notion of obscenity in the country and not publish anything that violates that standard. The net effect is that the rights of citizens in every other location are impaired." And Dershowitz: "Any community can act as the censor of any other community—that's small-town censorship." If *Screw* is illegal in Paw Paw, Michigan, you see, it will be impossible or unprofitable to publish it in New York, and the mind of every American is manacled. One might as well argue that the remaining dry counties in Kansas inexorably will bring Prohibition back to New York. Actually it is the "libertarian" forces who are battling to impose a single rule everywhere— and who, in the name of "individual" rights, would deny citizens the right to act as a community for certain purposes. As usual, their demand for "freedom" is for a kind of freedom that in fact must come at the expense of a structural principle of real freedom: the principle of federalism.

By all means *do* shed a tear for the First Amendment— not because it is threatened in Kansas, but because it is expounded in the nation's top law schools by such minds as those of Messrs. Stone and Dershowitz.

THE "FILTHY WORDS" DECISION [4]

In its final decision of the year, the Supreme Court upheld the right of the Federal Communications Commission to reprimand the Pacifica Foundation for having broadcast,

[4] Article from *America*. 139:44–5. Jl. 29, '78. Reprinted with permission of America Press Inc., 106 West 56th Street, New York, N.Y. 10019. © 1978. All rights reserved.

at 2:00 in the afternoon, George Carlin's 12-minute monologue on "Filthy Words." The monologue, originally delivered to a live audience in a California theater, satirizes
society's objection to the public use of seven particular words
describing sexual and excretory activities and organs. By
repeatedly and deliberately ringing the changes on these
words, Carlin greatly amused his audience and made the
whole subject as silly as it really is.

Unfortunately, the Pacifica Foundation acquired a tape
of the monologue and broadcast it in the early afternoon
on one of its radio stations. A man, driving with his young
son, heard the broadcast and complained to the FCC. The
commission forwarded the complaint to the Pacifica Foundation, which defended its right to broadcast the monologue.
The commission disagreed with the foundation and issued
a declaratory order holding that Pacifica could have been
the subject of administrative sanctions because of the broadcast. The FCC advised Pacifica that the complaint had been
made part of the foundation's file, and that, if further complaints were received, the FCC would then decide which,
if any, administrative sanctions should be imposed.

The Supreme Court upheld the FCC's reprimand by a
5–4 vote. All nine justices agreed that the monologue was
not obscene; they split on the question of whether the FCC
has statutory authority to impose sanctions on stations that
broadcast "indecent" language that falls short of the obscene. The justices also disagreed among themselves about
the degree of protection provided by the First Amendment
to language that is "patently offensive," as judged by contemporary community standards.

Despite these disagreements, five members of the Court
reached a sufficient consensus to establish a majority rationale that provides some guidance for both the FCC and the
broadcasters. Under that rationale, stations will be subject
to administrative sanctions (such as monetary penalties,
short-term license renewals or license revocations) if they
broadcast, at a time when it is likely that there will be many
children in the audience, material that is as patently offen-

sive to commonly held convictions about propriety in public speech as was the Carlin monologue. As Mr. Justice John Paul Stevens pithily put it in his opinion for the Court: ". . . when the Commission finds that a pig has entered the parlor, the exercise of its regulatory power does not depend on proof that the pig is obscene."

I SAY LOCK 'EM UP [5]

The conviction of *Hustler* publisher Larry Flynt, like that of porn star Harry Reems a few months before, sent shudders through American civil libertarians. Reems especially was thought to have received unfair treatment: he was prosecuted under a conspiracy law, when he had merely performed before a camera, in all innocence, a few routine unnatural acts, leaving the real scheming to the producers and distributors. Both Reems and Flynt also got the sympathy that often attaches to those who have the misfortune to be punished under old laws seldom invoked.

Some of their defenders, not content to seek redress for the two individuals, warned of dire consequences to the whole Republic. "Today Harry Reems, tomorrow Helen Hayes," said Warren Beatty. (As of this writing, Miss Hayes is still on the streets.) A group of well-known liberals signed an ad on behalf of "Larry Flynt: American Dissident," although *Harper's* editor Lewis Lapham, having tardily made the acquaintance of Flynt's product, withdrew his name, and others questioned the propriety of Flynt's attempt to ride the coattails of Solzhenitsyn.

But it was left to the New York *Times*, headquarters of judicious alarmism, to hit the crystal-shattering high C with an article in its Sunday magazine asking "Has the First Amendment Met Its Match?" The obvious import of that question was that it would be a terrible thing indeed if the

[5] Article, entitled "I Say Lock 'Em Up, Spank Them, and Send Them Home," by M. J. Sobran Jr., senior editor. *National Review.* 29:712–13. Je. 24, '77. Reprinted by permission of *National Review*, 150 E. 35th St., New York, NY 10016.

answer was yes. Never mind why. The automatic and un-
critical veneration accorded the First Amendment (but not
the Second, or the Third, or . . .) is downright touching in
an age when most people scoff at Mother and the flag. Surely
no other public value has won such secure *sacrabovinitas*.

Not only is the First beyond criticism, and critical
thought: obscenity is widely regarded as the acid test of our
commitment to freedom of expression. . . . "I am not sure
that *Hustler* is what Jefferson had in mind," quipped Lapham. Evidently not. But does that matter? Flynt's defenders,
after all, contend that the First Amendment commits us to
an ideal of liberty so strict that the pornographer inescapably enjoys the same latitude as the philosopher—whether
we personally like it or not.

One might retort along the lines of Mr. Bumble that if
the First Amendment says *that*, then the First Amendment
is a ass, and a idiot, and we'd be better off without it. France
and England don't have it, and they are generally recognized as free countries, despite their various restrictions on
speech, the press, and access to electronic communications.
Desirable or not, their example exposes as cant the notion
that the slightest infraction of free expression poses a threat
to Helen Hayes—a notion parallel to the old warning that
Social Security laws would lead inexorably to Communism.
No need to be Bumblesque about it, but it may sober up the
discussion a little to acknowledge that liberty can be reasoned about, like any other large topic, without recourse to
the bogus prophecy. Liberty is a solid, not a gas.

The obscenity problem is delicate in itself, and needs no
further clouding; but that, alas, is the effect of the general
confusion over the meaning of freedom of speech and of the
press. Few people ask the obvious question: *In what sense*
is freedom of speech a "right"? It is not an unqualified
moral right, for you obviously have no right to lie, to insult,
to incite malice, to betray confidences, and so forth; nor a
social right, for other people have the right to punish what
they deem your intolerable utterances by applying such
extra-legal sanctions as ostracism (polite society properly ex-

cludes Jew-baiters, for instance); nor a legal right, for the law provides penalties for libel, fraud, false advertising, inciting to riot, and other injurious forms of speech; nor a political right, for, as Burke put it, it is absurd to demand of civil society "rights" inimical to the existence and survival of civil society. (Some people try to evade this last objection by arguing that the polity always profits, "ultimately" at least, by tolerating free discussion. That is merely a disguised form of the bogus prophecy. It implies that speech—tacitly identified, by the way, with "discussion"—is always beneficent, never destructive, in its effects. Unfortunately, happy endings are never inevitable; not even in parliamentary situations.)

Most of these restraints on speech do no more than embody the natural recognition that speech, like other kinds of human conduct, is limited by the various contexts in which it occurs. Such restraints do not mean that we are unfree; rather they define the *kind* of freedom we enjoy. The existence of speed limits on our highways has never caused anyone to think his freedom to travel was seriously impaired; nor did the lowering of the upper limit to 55 miles per hour lead Americans to fear that they would soon be forced to stay home. Even Warren Beatty could see through that one. But there is one more important sense in which free speech is thought to be an unqualified right.

That of course is historical. As Americans, it is contended, we enjoy a unique guarantee of total freedom of utterance. So committed was Justice Hugo Black to this idea that he even argued that libel laws should be abolished (though it should be noted that his reasons were principled, not alarmist: he never said that failing to abolish them would finally tear down every other freedom, only that the First Amendment would reach full flower if they *were* abolished).

Unfortunately, this rests on a misreading of the First Amendment. As every schoolboy used to know, the Bill of Rights was a limitation on the new Federal Government. Hence it begins, "*Congress* shall make no law . . ." That merely ensured that central power would not be used in such a way as to abridge—what? Not a vague "freedom of expression," but "*the* freedom of speech, or of the press"—that is, freedoms already existent, and in the forms in which they were already known, including the limitations already defining them. *The* freedom of speech and of the press, as known to the young states, was far from absolute: not only were lewd and libelous utterances (among others) subject to criminal penalties; in many localities, a woman might be put in the stocks or pillory as a "common scold." The Fourteenth Amendment and subsequent Supreme Court decisions have substantially expanded the original meaning of the First, but the Court has never ruled that obscenity laws as such are unconstitutional. All-out libertarianism may yet find some strong arguments; it cannot pretend to much of a historical pedigree. (Most people who invoke the First Amendment cannot even quote it accurately, let alone say what it meant and did in 1791. The facts are scrupulously recounted and interpreted in Leonard Levy's *Freedom of Speech and Press in Early American History: Legacy of Suppression* [1964]. As the subtitle—originally the title—suggests, Professor Levy, a conscientious libertarian, was disappointed by his own findings. Nonetheless, he has given us a tonic antidote to constitutional idolatry.)

Like free speech, obscenity is an idea that seems to put a crimp in the minds of ordinarily straight thinkers. Columnist William Raspberry responded to Flynt's conviction by ridiculing the very concept of "obscenity," adding that Flynt and his customers should be permitted to do what they like in private, "as long as they don't force their filth on me."

That sounds reasonable, except of course that Flynt's campaign is largely an assault on public standards of decency, as witness the very covers of his magazines. He and his competitors show not the slightest restraint about "forcing their filth" on everyone, everywhere. (By the way, Mr. Raspberry fails to explain how he distinguishes "filth," which he recognizes on the street, from "obscenity," the definition of which he thinks eludes philosophers.) If obscenity is a meaningless concept, then there are no grounds for forbidding Mr. Flynt to put Mr. Reems on a billboard. We must of course distinguish between what is permissible in private and what is tolerable for public exhibition (both in confined areas, for voluntary, paying spectators, and in open areas, where passersby can't avoid it). But we may as well face it: either we acknowledge objective standards of sexual propriety, along with the concomitant possibility of restricting even private consensual acts; or we abandon such standards, and get the billboards—leaving Mr. Raspberry, if he wishes to avoid filth, with the option of walking down the street with his eyes closed.

Maybe it is impossible to prohibit obscenity as such, but that does not make it necessary to abandon the concept. We can't ban injustice as such either, but that truism does not stop us from passing specific laws animated by an ideal of justice not easily codified. It is obviously feasible to specify what organs and what acts may not be put on display. We still prosecute the man who shows his penis to a little girl in the park, even to a consenting little girl; and if that is not in some sense an obscene act, her consent is immaterial: we have Flasher Lib. (Courtesy of William Raspberry?)

What is needed is a systematic explication of the idea of obscenity, with reference to the related ideas of privacy, sexual morality and symbolism, and the authority of social convention. The word itself may never regain the consensus of particular reference it once had for, say, little Protestant communities, in which a jury could quickly agree on whether or not the exhibition of a woman's breasts constituted a punishable affront to decency; but this is all the more reason for a careful general definition.

Nor is there any reason why local communities could not set their own standards. Publishers and distributors would simply have to determine where their wares might be sold, just as liquor companies must learn to coexist with occasional dry counties, and makers of deodorants are now learning where aerosol spray cans are outlawed. That this might in a marginal case put a publisher out of business is too bad, but beside the point. That enough "benighted places" (the phrase is from former Justice William O. Douglas, who was more confident of his ability to determine "benightedness" than "obscenity") could result in making it unprofitable to publish *Ulysses* is regrettable, but, after all, one of those little chances we take in life: specifically, it is the risk entailed by self-government. Localized government may result in local benightment, but no more than centralized government produces general benightment. Get enough backward voters in Georgia, and you wind up with Governor Carter. Get enough backward voters in the United States, and you wind up with President Carter. (The point may be strengthened, for some readers, by substituting the name of Richard Nixon.)

Perhaps obscenity should, for measured reasons, be tolerated. But sloganeering about free speech, or simply dismissing the notion of decency—which is nothing but the idea of privacy applied to public situations—will not do. Free public discussion is a good, even a precious thing, but that is distinct from the commercial display of the human body, and moreover (to judge from the quality of the discussion of the Flynt case) isn't all it is cracked up to be. The combination of Flynt himself and the torrent of sheer clichés he has inspired is enough to give the First Amendment a bad name.

How debasing it is to liberty when we equate its fruition with its exercise by the cynical. Those who fought for freedom of speech did so *not* because they were indifferent to what might be done with it, but because they held and cherished an ideal of civil conversation. The "exceptions" to absolute license, scandalous though they may be to Warren Beatty, were not an anomalous residue of suppression; they were part of the rule itself. Freedom was good so far as it tended to promote a certain *kind* of utterance—and of course this meant tolerating a good deal of speech that fell short of, and even violated, the norms of civility. It is prudent to make distinctions; and they must be applied with prudence. But an undistinguishing libertarianism, refusing to prefer the philosopher over the smut-peddler, or the democrat's error over the totalitarian's lie, is as confused as an anarchism that would insist that we are truly free only when we abolish all law. A society in which parliamentary disciplines are abrogated will soon descend into a shouting contest. A society that observes those disciplines deserves its liberty.

OBSCENITY—FORGET IT [6]

There is, rather suddenly, a resurgence of interest in the legal field that goes by the name "obscenity." Not that it ever lacked for interest. The conjunction of sex and politics is irresistible. But now there is more than interest; there is consternation—on the part of those who fear for our morality, on the part of those who fear the First Amendment will founder on the convictions of Harry Reems and Larry Flynt.

I suggest we abandon the word obscenity. I do not mean that the law should ignore all the many and varied things that legislatures and courts have tried to deal with under this rubric. My suggestion rather is that we drop the word and turn our attention to the social interests actually involved. Then, perhaps, some sensible law-making and law enforcement will follow.

The law is verbal art. It depends for its effectiveness on compact, muscular words; overgrown, flabby words are useless in the law, worse than useless—confusing, damaging. "Obscene" as a description of the morally outrageous or the intellectually monstrous continues to be useful (and generally has little to do with sex). "Obscene" for legal purposes should be discarded altogether. It carries an impossible burden of passionate conviction from both sides of the question. And it diverts attention from real issues. The present litigation over what is called obscenity involves serious public concerns which the word obscures and distorts.

Draw back a bit. Exactly eleven years ago a battle against

[6] Article by Charles Rembar, New York lawyer and author of *The End of Obscenity* and *Perspective*. *Atlantic Monthly*. 239:37–41. My. '77. Copyright © 1977, by The Atlantic Monthly Company, Boston, MA. Reprinted by permission.

literary censorship came to a close. What had been censored, for three hundred years, was called, in law, obscenity. Obscenity in its traditional sense—impermissible writing about sex, impermissible either because of what it described or because of the words that were used—was at an end. Writers would be able to write as they pleased on the subject of sex, and use whatever language they thought best. They would no longer have to keep a mind's eye on the censor; they could pay full attention to their art and ideas. The field of legal struggle would move to other forms of expression—films, the stage, television, photography.

So much has changed in the last eleven years that one who had not lived through earlier times would find the freedom that writers now enjoy unremarkable. Yet in the few decades just then ended, such works as Dreiser's *An American Tragedy*, Lillian Smith's *Strange Fruit*, and Edmund Wilson's *Memoirs of Hecate County* had been the subjects of successful criminal prosecution. Recently, in contrast, there has been no suppression of books at all. Obscenity prosecutions are now directed at motion pictures and stage performances and magazines (the last not for their words but for their pictures).

The contest concluded in 1966 was essentially between accepted sexual morality (which sought to govern what was expressed as well as what was done) and the guaranties of the First Amendment. The books declared obscene had been attacked and suppressed for a double reason: because, in the view of the ruling group, they induced immoral behavior, and because their open publication was immoral in itself. The very first brief in the very first case of the series that changed the law—the trial of *Lady Chatterley*—put the question this way: "Should the courts chain creative minds to the dead center of convention at a given moment in time?" Conventional sexual morality was what was meant and understood.

Whether or not you agree with the view of those who sought to preserve morality by limiting speech and writing, obscenity as a legal concept was a fair description of what they objected to. It had been attacked as indefinable, but it was no harder to define, no vaguer, perhaps less vague, than other concepts the law engages every day—"the reasonable person," for example, or "good faith," not to mention "fair trial." Its scope had varied over the years, but that is true of all legal concepts. The important point for present purposes is that however uncertain its boundaries, the legal term "obscenity" served a specific social goal.

The real difficulty—which had not been suggested as a difficulty until the twentieth century was well under way— was that the pursuit of the goal might run afoul of the First Amendment. Among the things settled in the series of cases that culminated in the *Fanny Hill* decision was that the attempt to enforce these moral standards through anti-obscenity laws must yield to the Amendment.

The First Amendment protects speech and press. Not all speech and press; there are some exceptions—information helpful to an enemy in wartime, for example, or fraudulent statements to induce the purchase of stocks and bonds. (And even speech and press protected by the First Amendment remain subject to some regulation. You may not, without municipal permission, choose to hold a meeting in the middle of a busy street and proclaim your thoughts while traffic waits.) But obscenity is no longer an exception to freedom of speech and press in the traditional meaning of those terms. And it ought not be an exception for speech and press more broadly defined—communication in general.

"Suppress," however, means throttle altogether. Even the liberal justices of the present Supreme Court, the dissenters from the Burger view, have allowed that expression can be in certain ways restricted. That is, the citizen who has something he wishes to communicate may not be silenced completely—he can be as obscene about it as he likes —but the flow of his expression can be channeled. These liberal justices have said that the First Amendment is not infringed by anti-obscenity laws that seek to safeguard children or to prevent the infliction of unwanted displays on a captive audience.

Another limitation on expression occurs when expression is mixed with action. Consider the poor soul arrested for indecent exposure. No doubt he has something to communicate, if it is only "look at me," but what he does is also an act, and there is no possibility the Supreme Court would preclude the prosecution of the flasher on the theory that he is only invoking First Amendment rights.

The most libertarian of our justices, Hugo Black and William Douglas, carved out and set aside "action brigaded with expression." Even while they were advancing their thesis that the First Amendment must be given an "absolute" construction—that speech and the press must be subject to no restraint whatever—they said that when behavior was involved, a different question was presented. The situation must be analyzed to determine which element, action or expression, can be said to dominate. The control of conduct has never been restricted by the First Amendment. Indeed, the control of conduct is the primary business of government. The prosecution of Harry Reems, actor in *Deep Throat*, poses an interesting problem. The film was made in Florida, where the actors performed their acts; Reems was prosecuted in Tennessee, a place where the film was shown. Behavior more than expression? In Florida maybe, it seems to me; in Tennessee, no.

It is in these three fields that legitimate problems remain —the protection of children, the unwilling audience, and action mixed with expression. In each instance, however, we would do better to use legal concepts other than obscenity.

When we are dealing with behavior rather than expression, the only question is what kind of behavior we ought to regulate—whether, for instance, any kind of private sex between (or among) consenting adults should be prohibited. The answer does not involve the First Amendment. Laws controlling conduct rather than communication, as we have seen, do not infringe freedom of speech or press.

The most prominent current topic on which this distinction may help arises from municipal efforts to deal with the ugly sore of commercial sex—Boston's delimitation of its

"Combat Zone," Detroit's recently upheld dispersal ordinance, New York's attempt to restore the center of Manhattan to something like what it used to be. Prostitution, with its corollary crimes, is present. So are pornographic bookstores. So are hard-core films. We tend to treat them as though they all present a single legal problem. They do not. Prostitution is behavior, not expression. Whether it should be licensed, or simply decriminalized, or continue to be prosecuted, is a troubling question, but it has nothing to do with the First Amendment. Prostitution is clearly on the conduct side of the conduct–expression divide.

But films and books and magazines are on the other side, and here the other concepts enter, and another distinction. We must distinguish between the willing audience and the captive audience. You can say or write or show what you please, but only to those who are willing to listen, or read, or view. *Tropic of Cancer* printed in volume form is one thing; *Tropic of Cancer* blared out by bullhorn in a public square is quite another. The right to express oneself is not the right to intrude expression on those who do not want it.

Privacy has been recognized as a constitutional right. It is actually a cluster of rights, one of which is the right to be let alone. Exhibition inside theaters is in this sense private; no one is compelled to enter. The same for books and magazines; no one is forced to read them. But once the stuff spills onto the streets—on theater marquees or posters, in storefront windows or newsstand displays—the privacy of those outside is assaulted. The liberty of those who like pornography is not inconsistent with the liberty of those who don't. Neither should be constrained by law—the one denied the means to gratify his voyeurism, the other forced to share it. If the people wish to forbid public exhibition of certain kinds—exhibition which dismays some of those who are trying to enjoy their clear right to use the streets and sidewalks free of assault—there is no First Amendment reason that ought to stand in the way. It need not be labeled obscenity. What is thrust upon the passerby can be regulated because the citizens feel it is disagreeable or offensive or unhealthy—that is, if there are enough such citizens so that under our democratic processes they constitute a majority.

Privacy is the modern idea that inheres in this situation. An ancient legal idea reinforces it. It is the traditional and useful and sensible idea of nuisance. In New York, 42nd Street constitutes a public nuisance. No need to cogitate and strain over whether the displays are obscene. Let the movies be shown in the theaters, but restrict, if the voters wish, what appears on their marquees. Let the magazines be sold—let the pimps to masturbators think of themselves as publishers—but keep their product off the front of newsstands.

These paragraphs may raise two questions in the reader's mind. I have stressed, in other writings, that the safeguards of the First Amendment are designed for minority views: there would be no need for the amendment if all we wanted to protect was what the majority deemed acceptable. Hence the references above to "a majority" and to "what the people wish" may seem, if one reads too quickly, rather odd. The answer is that these paragraphs deal with situations to which, if the prescription is followed, the First Amendment does not extend. And I am referring to the kind of thing at which anti-obscenity laws are aimed, not to political speech.

The second question is, How do you do it? How do you provide for the permission to publish and the prohibition of display—the permission to exhibit in closed theaters and the control of what is out on the street? Fifty difficult hypotheticals can be rattled off in fifty minutes. But this is true of almost any statutory regulation. Laws are hard to apply and enforce; this does not mean we should not have them. When, for instance, does merger become monopoly? When does an efficient business arrangement become restraint of trade? The fact that these are large, perplexing questions, which spawn thousands of more perplexing little questions, does not mean we ought not have our antitrust laws. To deal with all the legal questions my proposals might bring in their train would require a legal treatise. This short piece is necessarily elliptical, and I am not trying to draft the statutes. But I believe such statutes can be drawn, and enforced with fair success.

Finally, child abuse. Although there is disagreement about *how* their cultural environment affects the emotional development of children, there is consensus that the environment is a powerful factor. (If the reader of this piece has a liberal bent, it may help his thinking on the subject to concentrate not on sex but on violence.) A legislative effort to shield the child from certain representations of sex (or violence) does not, in the view of the justices most concerned with freedom, infringe the First Amendment. Nor does the legislature have to prove that ill effects inevitably flow from what it prohibits. Since the First Amendment is not involved, the only constitutional inhibition is the due process clause, and there the test is not whether the legislature is absolutely right, or even sure of the efficacy of its statute. The test is whether there is a rational basis for its concern, and whether what it tries to do about it is not altogether foolish. The established constitutional formula for testing legislation against the due process clause is that it not be "arbitrary and unreasonable."

It is not arbitrary or unreasonable for the legislature to conclude that inducing children to engage in sexual activity can harm them. Nor is it arbitrary or unreasonable to prohibit the photographing of children who have been induced to do so, or to interdict the publication and sale of magazines in which the photographs appear. The publisher and the seller are principals in the abuse. Without them, it would not occur.

There is also abuse of children in another situation—where the child is audience rather than subject. Here television is the prime subject of concern; children are overexposed to what comes through the tube. It will not do to say the family should exercise control. Pious introductions warning of "mature theme" and advice to exercise "parental guidance" are stupid, unless they are cleverly meant to be self-defeating, and in either event they are revolting. If the children are not watching, the caveat has no purpose; if the children are watching, the caveat is a lure. This is obscenity in its larger, nonlegal sense.

Our habits have come to the point where the family in the home is the captive audience par excellence. Neither the child's own judgment nor, as a practical matter, the authority of parents can make effective choices. A legislative attempt to control the content of television programs that had a reasonable basis in the aim to safeguard children would not violate the Constitution.

Our most liberal justices have pointed out that the world of the child is not the world of the adult, and efforts to limit expression have a special place where children are concerned. (Broadcasters who resist control are making a claim to be free in the sense the right wing often uses—freedom to exploit monopolies.) Here again the standard is not obscenity.

Apart from these three fields, the First Amendment demands that we must put up with a lot of what is disagreeable or even damaging. The point made by feminists—that porno films and magazines demean and exploit women—is a strong one. (It is even stronger than they think: the things they object to demean and exploit all people.) But the First Amendment, I believe, requires that we let the material be produced and published. So long as expression is involved and intrusion is not, and there is no question of child abuse, our arguments should be addressed not to the courts but to the producers and sellers of entertainment. That is not an entirely futile effort. The public can be affected by these arguments, and it is the public after all that makes the selling of entertainment a profitable venture. To the extent that these arguments do not prevail, we must accept the fact that the freedoms guaranteed by the First Amendment are costly freedoms. Very costly. Worth the cost, I would say.

The First Amendment has lately had to contend with more than its old enemies. The effectiveness of any law—including our fundamental law, the Constitution—depends on the people's perception of it. The prime example of a

law destroyed because too many saw it as fatuous was Prohibition. Freedom of the press has trouble enough as an
operating concept—as distinguished from an incantation—
without having to defend itself from those who like to call
themselves its friends.

The voguish furor about anti-obscenity laws diminishes
the public perception of the First Amendment in two ways.
One is the silliness—calculated or naive—of so many who
rush to grab and wave the First Amendment banner. Lawyers defend topless bars with phrases out of *Areopagitica*.
Blind to the fact that all constitutional law is a matter of
degree, an actor solemnly proclaims: "Today Harry Reems,
tomorrow Helen Hayes." Fatheadedness rarely helps a cause.

The other source of debilitation is a sort of constitutional
imperialism. Freedom of expression is not our only liberty.
It is, to my mind, our most important liberty, the basis of
all others. But it is part of an entire structure. It is entitled
to no imperium; it must democratically live with other guaranties and rights.

The First Amendment has serious work to do. Invoked
too often and too broadly, it can grow thin and feeble. The
restrictions I suggest are minimal, and specific, and—with the
anachronistic concept of obscenity discarded—they allow
more freedom than the courts have granted up to now. And,
I think, they may help to avoid a dangerous dilution of First
Amendment guaranties.

Postscript

People to whom I have broached the idea submitted in
this essay have asked about its evolution. What goes on in
the mind of a lawyer who once attacked obscenity laws so
hard and now suggests legal restrictions on some of the
things that are commonly called "obscene"?

A novelist, speaking from the feminist side, reads me an
essay she is doing. It mentions "Charles Rembar, the attorney who escorted Lady Chatterley and Fanny Hill to
their triumphant American debuts, thereby unwittingly

spreading his cloak—and ours—in the muddy path for a pack of porno hustlers." Not *unwittingly*, I say, and then I quote from *The End of Obscenity:*

> The current uses of the new freedom are not all to the good. There is an acne on our culture. Books enter the best-seller lists distinguished only by the fact that once they would have put their publishers in jail. Advertising plays upon concupiscence in ways that range from foolish to fraudulent. Theatre marquees promise surrogate thrills, and the movies themselves, even some of the good ones, include "daring" scenes—"dare" is a child's word—that have no meaning except at the box office. Television commercials peddle sex with an idiot slyness.

Among the lesser detriments of the new freedom is the deterioration of the television situation comedy, an art form that has not been altogether bad and has had, indeed, high moments. It suffers now from a blue-brown flood of double-meaning jokes, stupidities accompanied by high cackles from the studio audience. (How do they gather those people? Or is it only a Moog synthesizer?) On the other hand, among the more important benefits are the intelligent discussions, on television, of subjects that could not be publicly discussed before; it is difficult to remember, but a documentary on birth control could not have been aired some years ago. Also, just possibly, a new and wonderful trend in journalism: It may no longer be feasible to sustain a bad newspaper by loading it with leers; since sex stories are much less shocking today, the old circulation formula may be hard to work.

Do the suggestions I make jeopardize the freedom won eleven years ago? I think not. In fact, in terms of what may be suppressed, they expand it. The freedom was won for the printed word; for other forms of expression, the decisions carried implications of greater liberty than had theretofore been enjoyed, though not as complete as writers would enjoy. In arguing the cases, I said that not all media were the same, and called attention to the points that underlie the approach outlined above—the protection of children, the problem of action mixed with expression, and one's right not to be compelled to constitute an audience. (Don't pluck my sleeve as I am passing by, stop poking your finger on my chest; freedom includes freedom from your assailing my senses—these are fair demands that books don't interfere with.)

All that is new in my position is the proposal that we come to the end of obscenity in another sense and turn our attention to the things society may rightfully care about.

The proposal is made with the thought that it can make the First Amendment stronger.

II. THE FIRST AMENDMENT'S WIDE NET

EDITOR'S INTRODUCTION

A remarkably varied group of issues—some seemingly un-related—always manages to fall into the wide net of First Amendment concern. The previous chapter discussed ob-scenity cases; this chapter covers a waterfront of cases and issues involving freedom of religion, individual privacy versus the press, television's special liability to legal re-straints, government secrecy, and the constitutionality of campaign laws.

The first article in this section, "Everybody Has the Right to Be Wrong" by Jean Caffey Lyles, as associate editor of the *Christian Century,* brings up a number of issues re-lated to a "deprogramming" case recently decided in the Cal-ifornia Superior Court but destined for appeal. One of the essential issues in this controversial case is whether the fol-lowers of Reverend Moon (or any cult, for that matter) are accorded the same First Amendment guarantee of the free exercise of their religion as those who call themselves Bap-tists, Jews, or Episcopalians.

Turning from freedom of religion to freedom of the press, the second article, from the New York *Times Maga-zine,* "The Press, Privacy and the Constitution" by Floyd Abrams, a noted attorney and civil libertarian, gives a sur-vey of cases in which journalistic rights have come into direct conflict with the privacy rights of both individuals and the United States government.

Describing a First Amendment case of very different order, Karl E. Meyer, in a *Saturday Review* article entitled "Television's Trying Times," relates the facts surrounding a primetime broadcast by NBC, which was the subject of an $11 million negligence suit. NBC's defense maintained in part that if the suit were successful "The First Amendment and society's right to the creativity of its members would be crippled."

The fourth article, "Our All Too-Timid Press," by columnist Tom Wicker argues that the press must take a more active, independent, and adversary position toward the government—a position safeguarded by the First Amendment—if it is to preserve its freedom to publish what and when it wants.

Next, in "A Secretive Security" reprinted from the *Center Magazine,* David Wise conducts a discussion by several distinguished journalists and lawyers on the "conflict in our society between First Amendment values and the values we associate with national defense and national security."

In the section's final article, "Two Theories of Press Freedom" reprinted from the New York *Times,* Floyd Abrams who represented NBC in the Niemi case (see page 64) discusses a Supreme Court decision on the constitutionality of a Massachusetts campaign law—a decision that brings up the issue of whether the press enjoys a special protection under the Constitution that individuals or other businesses do not.

EVERYBODY HAS THE RIGHT TO BE WRONG[1]

In most states, 18 is now the age at which a young person legally becomes an adult. But whether majority is attained at 18, 19 or 21, the dividing line is arbitrary. Young persons do not necessarily acquire common sense, good judgment and emotional maturity on schedule—nor, for that matter, financial independence. And parents are seldom ready to relinquish all parental control on their offspring's 18th or 21st birthday.

A recent article in the Milwaukee *Journal* describes the work of two professors at the University of Wisconsin–Milwaukee who are extending the literature of child-rearing and adolescent psychology to encompass an age group that

[1] Article entitled "Letting Go: Everybody Has the Right To Be Wrong," by Jean Caffey Lyles, associate editor. *Christian Century.* 94:451–3. My. 11, '77. Copyright 1977 Christian Century Foundation. Reprinted by permission from the May 11, 1977 issue of *The Christian Century.*

almost nothing has been written about: "the child from 18 to 25"—the "Not-Quite-Adult," or "NQA" for short. The prolonged dependence of young persons, with parents supporting children through graduate school and beyond, is a fairly recent phenomenon, but Emmy Lou and Quentin Schenk believe that the family has not completed its mission until this stage of ambivalence is successfully negotiated and independence is achieved. They are writing a book on the subject called *How to Let Go and How to Get Free*. Parents want to hang on to children, it seems, because once the nest is empty, they have to find new purposes for their own lives beyond the task of child-rearing. And many kids aren't struggling to break free because they're not ready to give up the generous allowance, use of the family car, home-cooked meals, rent-free quarters and laundry service. But here's the catch: "Anytime there is dependency, there is control. Parents would like dependency without the drain on their financial resources. Children would like financial support without control."

Looking at the matter of dependency and control from a different perspective, educator John Holt, a disciple of Ivan Illich (*Deschooling Society*), wrote a book a few years ago called *Escape from Childhood*, in which he called into question the whole "modern invention" of childhood as we know it in Western culture, and proposed a new manifesto of children's rights: "The rights, privileges, duties [and] responsibilities of adult citizens [should] be made *available* to any young person, of whatever age, who wants to make use of them." In other words, it would be up to the child to decide when he or she was ready to claim one or more of these rights. Holt's list includes (among others) the right to equal treatment before the law, the right to vote, work, earn money, own property, borrow money, "manage one's own education," travel, decide where to live and with whom, drive a car, use drugs, and "control one's own private sex life." This radical and largely impractical proposal raised hackles; but Holt also raised at least one question that needs to be taken seriously: "If we gave up our vested interest in children's dependency and incompetence, would they not much more quickly become independent and competent?"

And now, a third view of childhood: "The child is the child even though a parent may be 90 and the child 60." That remarkable statement could well have been uttered by the central figure in Mell Lazarus's comic strip "Momma"— that sharp-tongued epitome of well-meaning but obnoxious smother-love whose highest purpose in life is controlling her grown-up children's lives.

The statement above is in fact quoted from a court ruling of California Superior Court Judge S. Lee Vavuris, who on March 24 ordered five young-adult members of Sun Myung Moon's Unification Church—ranging in age from 21 to 25—returned to the custody of their parents for 30 days of "religious deprogramming."

There must be many a parent who would like to indulge the fantasy of having 30 days to "deprogram" an almost-grown son or daughter, to have just one more crack at instilling the old family values and rescuing the child from the evil grip of "peer-group influences" or whatever. The sentiment is by no means limited to parents whose kids have joined a bizarre religious cult. The Protestant parent whose child becomes Catholic, or the Jewish parent whose offspring converts to Christianity, might be equally distressed.

Other candidates for deprogramming might include the young person who has adopted a homosexual life style, the one who has taken up pot-smoking, the young man or woman contemplating interracial or interfaith marriage, the unmarried couple who are living together, the young marrieds who say they don't want to have children, the pregnant-but–unmarried daughter who says she's going to keep the baby, the youngster who is bent on entering an "unsuitable" profession. Of all the difficult demands of the craft of parenting, one of the hardest is the art of letting go— watching as the not-quite-adult offspring makes wrong choices, ignores parental advice, goes against parental standards. Catholic writer Sally Cunneen writes about "the second stage of motherhood, the one you were not prepared for." What's a parent to do when a grown-up child adopts a way of life unacceptable to mother and father? Can we stand back and allow a 21-year-old the right to mess up his own life? "No," say Ted Patrick and other professional deprogrammers, who have offered their services to the distraught parents of cult members.

"Cult-napping" and deprogramming efforts have been of questionable legality, but the "conservatorship" laws of California and other states seemed to some parents and their attorneys to offer a legal way to straighten out the minds of their misguided sons and daughters. "Conservators" are persons appointed to protect the interests of senile and other mentally incapacitated persons unable to manage their own affairs. When these laws have been applied to cult members, young people have, at their parents' request, been declared "incompetent" in private hearings, without benefit of counsel. In the recent San Francisco decision, Judge Vavuris, recognizing the controversial nature of the issue, held an open hearing, with counsel, and called for appellate review of his ruling—thus making it a test case.

The parents must decide "what is best for their child," said the judge in turning the Moonies over to their parents. "We are talking about the essence of civilization—mother, father and children. There's nothing like it. I know of no greater love than [that of] parents for their children, and I am sure they would not submit their children to harm."

Civil-libertarian groups predictably denounced the ruling and said it was sure to be reversed. Americans United for Separation of Church and State called it "a major defeat for religious liberty in the United States."

It will probably be three months or so before the three-judge appeals court issues a final decision on the constitutionality of using conservatorship to place cult members under parental control—the judges must first study the lengthy transcript of the 11-day hearing that led to Judge Vavuris's ruling. The appellate court did, however, stay the custody order, freeing the five Moonies. (It appeared that only one of the five would take advantage of his freedom:

three announced that they were no longer followers of Mr.
Moon and would submit to deprogramming; the fourth was
thought by her mother's attorney to be headed for the Freedom of Thought Foundation, a "rehabilitation center for
deprogrammed youth" in Tucson, Arizona.)

And the appeals court did give some hint of what its
final decision is likely to be by (1) indicating that it did not
agree that parents retain certain rights over their children,
(2) noting that adults have equal status in courts of law, and
(3) stating that conservatorship cannot be granted unless a
person is "incompetent and unable to care for himself." The
question raised by that last statement was left unanswered:
Can Moonies and other cult adherents, presumed victims of
coercion, brainwashing and mind control, be defined as "incompetent"?

At the Vavuris hearing the two sides addressed the question with arguments that seemed inconclusive or even irrelevant. The parents, for example, contended that the church
had turned their kids into "unquestioning zombies." The
evidence? They were "willing to stand for hours on the street
selling flowers to raise money they never saw again." (Following the logic of that premise, one might question the mental
fitness of those ultra-respectable Protestant women who are
willing to stand for hours at a church bazaar selling home-
made cakes, pies and craftwork to raise money they will
never see again after it is sent off to a denominational mis-
sions agency.) And if further evidence were needed, the
young people were now "abnormally cheerful." In their own
defense, some of the Moonies sought to demonstrate their
undiminished faculties by favoring the court with musical
performances or recitations of original poems. Readers of
newspaper accounts were mercifully spared critical reviews
of the Amateur Hour in Judge Vavuris's courtroom.

Were the Moonies "persuaded" or were they "coerced"?
"Converted" or "brainwashed"? Is deprogramming a violation of their civil liberties? Are "fringe groups," whatever
their questionable methods of attracting followers, to be
accorded the same religious freedom the US Constitution

guarantees to those more sensible folk who go for the standard brands like Catholic and Jew, Baptist and Episcopalian? There will doubtless be more court cases and appeals, possibly reaching to the Supreme Court, before the conservatorship question is finally settled.

Defending civil liberties on principle is one of those risky "strange bedfellows" enterprises, as any good card-carrying civil libertarian soon learns. One always seems to be defending the indefensible. In upholding freedom of expression the ACLU finds itself supporting television violence, free speech for Nazis maligning Jews, and for Ku Klux Klan members slurring blacks. A group of 84 New York writers, publishers and civil libertarians who signed a recent ad headlined LARRY FLYNT, AMERICAN DISSIDENT, sponsored by Americans for a Free Press, seemed, to the casual reader, to be equating the plight of the convicted skin-magazine publisher with that of dissident Soviet writers and artists. (Larry Flynt and Alexander Solzhenitsyn? *Hustler* and *Gulag Archipelago?* Strange bedfellows indeed!) Americans United and others who defend freedom of religion for Sun Myung Moon's Unification Church are accused of ignoring the clear and present dangers the Moon movement poses.

Nonetheless, there is a principle here of civil liberties. A court decision that bars parents from using conservatorship laws to gain legal control over their youngsters will probably not stop anguished parents from resorting to deprogramming illegally. But certainly a court ruling that provides for legally sanctioned kidnapping and deprogramming could set a dangerous precedent for the future of religious liberties in America.

Parents have 18 years to transmit their own religious and cultural values to their young, and most of them are not going to get that 30-day extension. There comes a time when the parent must let go and hope for the best. From that point on, young persons must begin to make their own decisions and shape their own value systems, even if they are radically at variance with those of their parents. If young adults are to be assured of their civil liberties, they must be given one other freedom: the right to make the wrong choice.

THE PRESS, PRIVACY AND THE CONSTITUTION [2]

A swift move jostles a would-be assassin's arm. The shot misses President Gerald Ford. Sara Jane Moore receives a life sentence. But what of Oliver Sipple, the ex-Marine who deflected her aim? He becomes an instant hero, but national publicity also reveals that he is a member of San Francisco's gay community. Now, almost two years after the assassination attempt, Sipple's suit against several newspapers for invading his privacy proceeds through the California courts.

The Sipple case has broad implications. It is one of a growing number brought against the press by people who claim that even true statements about themselves may not be published. And it exemplifies what has become the single most ominous threat to the First Amendment's guarantee of press freedom—the explosion of privacy law.

For the press, recent years have seen a general easing of a variety of legal threats. When it appeared that sky-high libel judgments against national newspapers and magazines by local juries might inhibit—and ultimately prohibit—coverage of the civil-rights movement of the 1950s, libel law was all but rewritten by the Supreme Court. The press was provided with constitutional protection even for the publication of false statements about public officials, so long as the press had not deliberately falsified or printed the statements with serious doubts as to their truth.

When an effort was made to prohibit publication of the Pentagon Papers, the Supreme Court speedily rejected it. When lower court judges issued a flood of gag orders against publication of material about pending criminal cases, the Supreme Court made it all but impossible for any such orders to be entered in the future. And when a state at-

[2] Article by Floyd Abrams, New York lawyer who has represented a number of First Amendment cases, and lecturer at Yale Law School. New York *Times Magazine*. p 11–13. Ag. 21, '77. © 1978 by The New York Times Company. Reprinted by permission.

tempted to force newspapers to publish material they chose
not to print, the Supreme Court unanimously rebuffed that
effort.

Not all recent decisions involving the press have been in
its favor. In the case of New York *Times* reporter Earl Cald-
well, the Supreme Court declined to grant journalists a right
to refuse to testify with respect to their confidential sources.
[See Farber case, Section III.] And in cases involving the
press's right to enter prisons to interview inmates, the Court
rejected the argument that the First Amendment provided
special rights of access for the press. But neither of these
areas, important as they are, approach that of privacy in
terms of the risks they pose.

Discussions of those risks have become the staple of conversation at gatherings of editors and those of lawyers familiar with the field. When editors of newspapers meet to
discuss the current state of the American press, the growth
of privacy law is invariably high on the agenda. And at an
American Bar Association meeting of a committee on free
speech and free press held earlier this month, all the lawyers
present agreed that the expansion of privacy law posed more
of a threat to the press than any other.

One threat involves the possible substitution of an official governmental view—of legislators or judges—for the
judgment of editors as to what is "newsworthy." Another is
that the more privacy cases are decided against the press,
the more the press will be inhibited in gathering news; as
a consequence, much important newsgathering may become
all but impossible.

In the end, the press is the surrogate for the American
public. Because that public today absorbs more news than
ever before, its dependence on journalists and broadcasters
is unprecedented. Thus, any balancing of the right of privacy against the right of the press to report—and the public's
need to know—is not merely a journalistic dilemma, but an
American dilemma.

Before 1890, there was no such concept in American
jurisprudence as privacy law. In that year, two young Bos-

ton lawyers, who had been roommates at the Harvard Law School and then law partners, published an article on privacy in the *Harvard Law Review*. One was Louis Brandeis, whose lustrous career on the United States Supreme Court began 26 years later; the other was Samuel Warren, a wealthy and socially prominent Bostonian.

The background of the article—probably the single most important one in all American legal history—is remarkable for its pettiness. Warren, not Brandeis, spurred its drafting. Married in 1883 to the daughter of a Massachusetts senator, Warren had become increasingly irritated by the descriptions in the Boston "yellow press" of parties given by the socially prominent couple. The article faithfully reflects the irritation of the upper classes at their social inferiors.

Gossip is published, so the article says, "to occupy the indolent." One effect of gossip is to "belittle" by "inverting the relative importance of things, thus dwarfing the thoughts and aspirations of a people." Since the very publication of gossip,

crowds the space available for matters of real interest to the community, what wonder that the ignorant and thoughtless mistake its relative importance. Easy of comprehension, appealing to that weak side of human nature which is never wholly cast down by the misfortunes and frailties of our neighbors, no one can be surprised that it usurps the place of interest in brains capable of other things.

Out of such nineteenth-century condescension, the law of privacy was born. But what, specifically, would it protect against? Brandeis and Warren had complained of the "obvious bounds of propriety and decency" being over-stepped and of "idle or prurient curiosity" being served. They had urged that individuals be permitted to recover money damages for such publications, that injunctions be issued in some cases and that it would "doubtless be desirable" for criminal statutes to be adopted to punish invasions of privacy. But what is "propriety"? And how is one to tell "idle" curiosity from news?

The law was slow in its efforts to answer these questions.

Brandeis and Warren had published their article in 1890.
By 1941, only eight states had recognized a right to sue for
what was characterized as invasion of privacy; by 1964, the
number of states was 31; now it is 47 (excluding only Rhode
Island, Nebraska and Wisconsin).

Some privacy claims are, quite literally, laughable. There
is the suit by a former boxer against Groucho Marx:
Groucho, during a "You Bet Your Life" show of the late
1940s, had said, "I once managed a fighter named Canvas-
back Cohen. I brought him here, he got knocked out, and I
made him walk back to Cleveland." The real Cohen sued,
alleging that Groucho's joke was an invasion of his privacy.
Like Groucho, the court sent Cohen walking.

Other claims, however, raise more serious questions as
to the scope and nature of privacy protection. Four types of
privacy cases have arisen through the years. One relates to
the truthful disclosure of "private" facts; this is illustrated
by the example of Oliver Sipple, the ex-Marine who saved
President Ford. Another involves what are claimed to be
physical intrusions or trespasses by the press in the course
of its newsgathering; this is exemplified by the case of a
medical quack named A. A. Dietemann, who sued *Life*
magazine for the manner in which it gathered facts in order
to expose him. The third type of privacy action has to do
with the right to sell one's own name or likeness; an example of this is that of Human Cannonball Hugo Zacchini,
who sued a television station for broadcasting his act. The
fourth category arises when the press is said to have placed
someone in a "false light" in the course of describing him;
this is illustrated by the so-called "Desperate Hours" case,
in which James Hill claimed a magazine article misrepre-
sented his family's experience while being held hostage by
criminals.

"Private" Facts

The day after the assassination attempt on President
Ford, members of San Francisco's gay community mentioned
to San Francisco *Chronicle* columnist Herb Caen that they

were "proud—maybe this will help break the stereotype." Caen's article of September 24, 1975, contained such a reference to Sipple. Then, when Sipple was pressed on the subject, he disclosed that he had been one of the "court" of an elected "emperor" of the gay community. Believing that reporting on Sipple's activities in San Francisco's thriving gay community was newsworthy, California newspapers published articles referring to those activities. Sipple's suit, in turn, claims that because of the articles about him, his parents and brothers and sisters in Ohio learned for the first time of his homosexual affiliations and, as a result, abandoned him.

Sipple's lawyer, John Eshleman Wahl, has rhetorically inquired whether, if Sipple had known "that saving the life of the President would subject his sex life to the speculation and scrutiny of the national news media," he would have chosen to save the President's life at all. "How, in the name of logic and justice," Wahl has urged, "does a discussion of Mr. Sipple's private sexual orientation have anything to do with his saving of the President's life? Obviously and clearly it does not—but it sells papers."

In reply to this, Los Angeles *Times* attorney Robert S. Warren and journalists on that newspaper have pointed to the newsworthiness of Sipple's affiliation with San Francisco's gay community—both because Sipple's act was so contrary to the stereotyped (now Anita Bryantized) view of homosexuals, and because it seemed for a time that President Ford might not publicly thank Sipple because he was gay. (Ford did.) Warren also points to Sipple's own disclosures of his participation in San Francisco's gay community, disclosures Sipple claims were made on some kind of off-the-record basis.

As the law has thus far developed, it is difficult to envisage the Los Angeles *Times* losing the Sipple suit. A recent case involving yet another Californian, who had asserted a privacy claim arising out of an article about him in *Sports Illustrated*, seems to assure this result. That case was brought by a champion body surfer named Michael Virgil whose hobbies (which he disclosed to a *Sports Illustrated* reporter) included eating spiders, putting out lighted cigarettes in his mouth and diving down flights of stairs to impress women. When *Sports Illustrated* published an article containing that information, Virgil sued. And lost.

In its opinion the United States Court of Appeals spelled out its view as to the law, a view which appears to reflect that of most other lower courts, but which the United States Supreme Court has not yet ruled upon. So long as a truthful description of private facts about a person in the news is "newsworthy," the Court of Appeals said, a newspaper may not be found liable for publishing them. What is *not* newsworthy? According to the court,

the line is to be drawn when the publicity ceases to be the giving of information to which the public is entitled and becomes a morbid and sensational prying into private lives for its own sake, with which a reasonable member of the public, with decent standards, would say that he had no concern.

Concluding that the disclosures published in *Sports Illustrated* about Virgil could not meet such a test, the District Court (to which the case was returned) dismissed Virgil's suit. As will happen, one may guess, to Sipple's suit because of the newsworthiness—whatever the taste—of the revelations about him.

But the dismissal of the Sipple suit, even if it occurs, will not diminish the risks posed by other such privacy suits and other findings by other judges or jurors as to what is—and what is not—newsworthy. The Sipple suit, like that of Virgil before it, raises a more critical issue than that of what is newsworthy: It is who should decide what is newsworthy.

There are some in the press and the bar who consider the victory of *Sports Illustrated* in the Virgil case a major one, precisely because of its conclusion that the revelations about Virgil were newsworthy. But it is far from that. For one thing, the test set forth by the court in the Virgil case contains language so vague ("morbid and sensational prying"), so open-ended ("a reasonable member of the public") and so subjective ("decent standards") that it makes it all but impossible to determine in advance what may be published and what not. What would a member of the public with "decent standards" say, for example, about publishing information about President Kennedy's amorous meanderings? Or about Margaret Trudeau's walks on the wild side? Or about the fact that Frank Hogan, when he ran for District Attorney of New York County, had cancer and was likely not to live out the entirety of his term? Or even about accurate reports of Samuel Warren's nineteenth-century cocktail parties?

Historically, decisions as to what is and is not "newsworthy" are precisely the ones made by editors, not judges. They are not always made well or responsibly. But, as Chief Justice Warren E. Burger (whose record in First Amendment cases involving the press is far more supportive than is generally recognized) has written:

> For better or worse, editing is what editors are for; and editing is the selection and choice of material. That editors—newspaper or broadcast—can and do abuse this power is beyond doubt, but . . . calculated risks of abuse are taken in order to preserve higher values.

Judges are, as well, government officials, and it is generally taken as one of the great gifts of the First Amendment that it puts all such officials out of the newsrooms, not in them. One New York columnist, for example, while denouncing a Federal judge for a widely publicized recent decision affecting middle- and lower-income people, mentioned the judge's Park Avenue address. As a result, the judge received a torrent of angry and sometimes threatening mail. Should the journalist have printed the judge's address? The argument against printing it is strong. But should a judge—any judge—be permitted to make such a decision?

In libel law—that body of law relating to the publication of defamatory falsehoods—it has historically and constitutionally been the case that so long as what was published was true there could be no recovery against the press for its publication. But in the branch of privacy law involved in Sipple's case, what the offended party in effect says is not that false things have been said about him, but that true things have been said which should have gone unsaid. To a high degree, all such claims thus involve delicate and difficult questions of taste, an area in which journalists hardly can claim to have any better judgment than the rest of us and in which they sometimes have far worse. Yet to permit judicial tastes—or those of other governmental officials with "decent standards"—to determine what may be printed is surely far more dangerous. That, if anything, is the lesson of our history.

Physical Intrusions

A. A. Dietemann was a disabled veteran who—as a court would later phrase it—"was engaged in the practice of dealing with clay, minerals, and herbs . . . simple quackery." On September 20, 1963, two *Life* magazine reporters visited Dietemann in his home—which was also the office for his quackery. One of the reporters, acting as if she were a patient, described imaginary cancer symptoms to Dietemann, who promptly responded by advising that the reporter had eaten some rancid butter 11 years, 9 months and 7 days prior to the examination. While Dietemann (who carried a wandlike object in his hand) spoke with his "patient," his words were carried by a small radio transmitter in the reporter's purse to a parked car outside the Dietemann home where another *Life* reporter, an assistant district attorney and an investigator for the California Department of Public Health listened. The second reporter in Dietemann's house also took photographs without Dietemann's knowledge.

As a result of this journalistic effort, Dietemann was arrested for practicing medicine without a license. *Life* photographers took pictures of the arrest, and two weeks later *Life* published an article entitled "Crackdown on Quackery," containing a photograph surreptitiously taken at Dietemann's home.

Dietemann pleaded nolo contendere to the charge. He then sued *Life* for invasion of privacy.

Dietemann's claims, of course, raised far different prob-

lems from Sipple's. The legal result in the case was written
in 1971 by the distinguished Federal judge Shirley Hufstedler. Her opinion, for herself and other members of the
United States Court of Appeals, concluded that Dietemann
could recover for the invasion of his house by the *Life*
reporters and that a $1,000 verdict rendered in his favor by a
jury (for injury to his "feelings and peace of mind") was
constitutionally permissible. According to the Court, Dietemann's "den was a sphere from which he could reasonably
expect to exclude eavesdropping newsmen." As for the argument of *Life* that the First Amendment protected its kind
of investigative journalism, Judge Hufstedler sharply responded that "the First Amendment has never been con-
strued to accord newsmen immunity from torts [civil wrongs]
or crimes committed during the course of newsgathering."

Yet the result in the case remains troubling. It is one
thing to say that as a general matter one's home is sacrosanct
from invasion by outsiders and that journalists are as responsible as the rest of us for illegal or improper eavesdropping,
just as they are for speeding or even jaywalking. It is quite
another to conclude that when a person passes himself off as
a doctor and uses his home as his office, journalists may not
act as prospective patients and record the illegal activities
that occur there.

Professor Alfred Hill, of Columbia Law School, has recently highlighted the difficulty raised by the Dietemann
verdict with the following hypothetical question. Suppose
that reporters infiltrate the highest Mafia councils, employ
hidden cameras and other surreptitious devices, and, as a
result, obtain and publish conclusive proof of major criminal activity of the Mafia, the police, prosecutors and other
officials at the highest government levels. If all that were so,
Hill asks, can it be that the exposed Mafiosi could recover
for breach of their *privacy*?

One solution to this issue might be for American law to
borrow one aspect of British law and permit a jury to conclude that, even though a physical intrusion by the press
had occurred, the publication so benefited the public that

no recovery should be permitted. This would permit newspapers willing to do so to risk some physical intrusion or deception of quacks or of Mafiosi while knowing that a jury might well reject the defense. (Most newspapers, in fact, do not engage, as a journalistic matter, in the kind of deception involved in the Dietemann case.)

This is hardly a tidy solution, since it leaves open the possibility of different jury verdicts in all but identical cases, and jury decisions based on the success or failure of the alleged intrusion by the press. But if cases such as Dietemann's are to continue to be heard at all, such an approach seems to strike a better balance than did the court in the Dietemann case itself.

Self-Promotion

At the county fair in Burton, Ohio, on September 1, 1972, the audience saw a renewed version of an old American tradition: a human cannonball who was projected out of a cannonlike object into a net 200 feet away. A local television station filmed the 15-second spectacle and broadcast it on its 11 P.M. news program. While the film was being shown, the newscaster described the act as follows:

This . . . now . . . is the story of a true *spectator* sport . . . the sport of human cannonballing. . . . In fact, the great Zacchini is about the only human cannonball around, these days. . . . Believe me, although it's not a *long* act, it's a thriller . . . and you really need to see it *in person* . . . to appreciate it. . . .

Ten months later, Hugo Zacchini—the cannonball himself—filed suit in the Ohio courts. He alleged that the right to show the film of his act belonged to him and that the television station, by showing the film, had invaded his privacy.

The kind of privacy law involved in Zacchini's case protects an entirely different interest from that involved in both the Sipple and Dietemann cases—the right of self-promotion or publicity, of selling one's own talent. Yet Zacchini's act was broadcast on a regularly scheduled news program, with no effort by the station at any commercial exploitation of the act. Who wins?

So far, Zacchini. In a 5-to-4 decision rendered on June 28, 1977, the Supreme Court, in an opinion written by Justice Byron R. White, concluded that the First Amendment does not "immunize the media when they broadcast a performer's entire act without his consent." Although states may decline to permit recovery in such cases if they wish, the White opinion concluded that there is no constitutional compulsion that they do so. The case was thus returned to the Ohio courts for them to decide whether Zacchini should recover anything.

Like so many decisions in the field of privacy, the Zacchini ruling raises about as many questions as it answers. As Justice Lewis F. Powell's dissent inquires, what is an "entire act" anyway? Just the shooting of Zacchini through the air? Or the fanfare, possibly stretching over several minutes, "all accompanied by suitably ominous commentary from the master of ceremonies"? What will the effect of the opinion be, Powell asks, on the reporting on television of events at local fairs, of sports competitions, such as a winning ski jump, or of showing a short—but whole—skit from a theatrical revue?

More broadly, Justice Powell's dissent contends that far from focusing on whether an "entire act" was broadcast, the appropriate question is what use the station made of the film footage. If the use is "for a routine portion of a regular news program," Powell urges that the First Amendment should protect a broadcaster from a Zacchini-type of suit in the absence of proof by the plaintiff that the broadcast was a "subterfuge or cover for private or commercial exploitation." Otherwise, he argues, the public will simply be left uninformed about information it is entitled to know.

Justice Powell's dissent highlights the difficulty now posed with respect to the broadcasting of certain newsworthy events. It is true that "entire" acts have rarely been broadcast as news anyway; they rarely are newsworthy and to that extent the Zacchini decision may have limited future effect.

But the question remains whether the public is well served by any notion of privacy that prevents them from observing events as newsworthy, if trivial, as that of Hugo Zacchini's flights.

"False Light"

In September 1952, three escaped convicts entered the suburban Pennsylvania home of Mr. and Mrs. James J. Hill and their five children. For the 19 much publicized hours that followed, the Hills were held captive in their own home. They were treated courteously and not molested or otherwise treated violently. Two of the three convicts were killed a few days later by the police in a wild shoot-out.

Based on the experiences of the Hills, Joseph Hayes wrote a best-selling novel, *The Desperate Hours*. The book added to the actual tribulations of the Hills certain incidents which had not occurred. It told of beatings of the father and son by the convicts and a verbal sexual insult to the daughter. When *The Desperate Hours* was made into a play, *Life* magazine transported some of the actors to the home where the Hills had been held hostage to take pictures.

One was of the son being manhandled by a convict; it was captioned "Brutish Convict." Another was of the daughter biting the hand of one of the convicts to force him to drop a gun; it was captioned "Daring Daughter." A third showed the father throwing his gun through the door after his "brave try" to free his family failed.

Hill (represented in the Supreme Court by Richard Nixon) sued *Life* under a New York privacy statute, claiming that the *Life* article had given the impression that the play mirrored the Hills' experience, something *Life* knew "was false and untrue." In its opinion, written by Justice William J. Brennan, Jr., the Supreme Court rejected the argument that liability for this kind of invasion of privacy could ever be imposed, even for false statements, "unless actual malice—knowledge that the statements are false or in reckless disregard of the truth—is alleged and proved. . . ."

It was a major press victory, but it appears to be one which will be limited to cases—like Hill's—in which individuals were portrayed in a "false light" and not to cases such as that of Sipple, Dietemann or Zacchini.

Cases such as those described illustrate some, but hardly all, of the mileposts which privacy has passed. But the risks of the rapid growth of privacy law are not limited to such cases. They include, as well, a wide range of state statutes adopted to protect privacy. These also directly threaten the ability of the public to learn significant facts which even Brandeis and Warren would have agreed do not constitute "gossip." In Rhode Island, for example, a statute has been adopted permitting destruction of misdemeanor records after completion of a sentence or probation and following a specified period of time with no convictions. In California and New Jersey, records of marijuana-law violators may be destroyed. In New York and Missouri, authorities will not release information about arrests that do not result in conviction. And in South Carolina, a bill is now under consideration which would require destruction of records when a person found guilty is pardoned.

All these laws are well intended. They reflect serious societal judgments that in many cases criminal records should be destroyed in order to avoid further harming those accused and not convicted, those convicted of minor crimes or those whose convictions have been expunged by pardons. These laws are supported by organizations usually sensitive to First Amendment concerns, such as the American Civil Liberties Union.

But the rapid spread of such laws is among the most troublesome developments of the privacy explosion. Not the least problem posed by such statutes is their interference with any ability of the press to scrutinize criminal justice agencies. Cases which are not pursued by the prosecution for political reasons or dismissed by the courts—either because of corruption or incompetence—could not be followed if arrest records were not available. Exposés in the press, such as the 1972 St. Louis *Globe-Democrat* series which dis-

closed traffic-ticket fixing in the city courts and which led
to the removal of two judges and the chief clerk and to
criminal indictments would be all but impossible to develop.

Similarly, scrutiny of a multiple arrest record of an individual who was not later convicted of any crimes may lead
to the conclusion that he had been unjustly persecuted, or,
perhaps, that some kind of favoritism had led to a failure
to convict an obviously culpable party. In either event,
society would benefit from exposure of the very information
such statutes seek to destroy.

The case against destruction of conviction records is, if
anything, even stronger. Courtrooms, after all, are public
property; trials, as the Supreme Court has observed, are
public events; and convictions are matters of the greatest
public consequence. The notion that an individual may be
duly accused, tried and convicted of a crime and that no
record may lawfully be kept on his conviction is Orwellian
in its implications. It involves the destruction of history, of
truth, in the name of privacy. It would even prohibit citizens from learning if a candidate for school-board president
—or United States President—had committed crimes which
bear directly on his capacity to serve in office.

In Britain, the situation is even more forbidding: There,
it is a crime to publish the fact of a prior conviction if an
individual has not served more than 30 months in prison
and has not been arrested again within seven years. Thus, if
an English equivalent of Spiro Agnew (if that can be imagined) should run for Parliament eight years after his felony
conviction, *no* mention could be made of the conviction
in the British press.

(A striking example of the differences between the British and American legal systems may be seen in the fact that,
because of its references to the Sipple case, this very article
would, under British law, constitute a contempt of court,
thus subjecting its author and the editor and publisher of
this newspaper to fines or jail sentences. Under British law,
all such references would have been illegal, since that case
is still before the courts—where it may remain for years.

Through American eyes, it surely seems a strange way for a free nation to function.)

There is another side to the rapid development of privacy law in recent years, one that is far more appealing and surely less threatening than that involving the press. It stems from the conclusion of the Supreme Court that, against abuses by the government itself, the Constitution affords significant privacy protection.

Once again, Brandeis is most to be credited—this time, more affirmatively—with the development of this body of law. In a stirring and subsequently much quoted 1928 dissenting opinion in a case involving government wiretapping, he observed that the makers of our Constitution had "conferred, as against the government the right to be let alone— the most comprehensive of rights and the right most valued by civilized men."

The Constitution itself was later held to afford privacy not only from direct government surveillance and intrusion but from governmental instrusions into a wide range of deeply personal decisions. These include the right to marry regardless of the race of one's spouse; the right to purchase contraceptives; the right to an abortion, and other decisions relating to family relationships and child rearing. In one recent decision of this type, Justice Brennan concluded: "If the right of privacy means anything, it is the right of the individual, married or single, to be free from unwanted governmental intrusions into matters so fundamentally affecting a person as the decision whether to bear or beget a child." In other areas, it is surprising that protection against government interference into deeply private decisions has not been extended still further. It remains inexplicable that the courts can continue to rule, as they have, that homosexuals may be subjected to criminal prosecution for sexual practices in private between consenting adults.

If anything, expansion rather than contraction of privacy law may be expected in the future. To the extent any such expansion relates to the protection of the individual from the government, Brandeis's eloquent 1928 formulation re-

mains the last word: To protect the "right to be left alone,"
he wrote, "every unjustifiable intrusion by the government
upon the privacy of the individual, whatever the means employed, must be deemed a violation of the [Constitution]."
To the extent privacy law is expanded so as to make it still
riskier or more difficult for the press to publish the truth, a
quite different conclusion may be drawn. It is now 87 years—
four score and seven—since Brandeis and Warren drafted
their article. Is it too late to say that they were wrong?

TELEVISION'S TRYING TIMES [3]

American television's time of trial is now upon us. In
every section of the country, at every level in the courts,
broadcasters have been brought before the bar, pitted
against those who wish to punish and restrain a medium that
has managed—for reasons good and bad—to provoke something close to a rebellion against programs that feature sex,
violence, or anything "controversial."

As a consequence, it is happy hunting for lawyers. No
charge against television seems too outlandish, given the
medium's pervasive influence and special status as a federally
licensed industry. A year ago, the networks were accused of
turning a Florida youth into a murderer. After a Miami jury
rejected the contention that Ronny Zamora, 15, was a victim of "involuntary television intoxication," his parents,
at their lawyer's urging, promptly filed a $25 million dam-
age suit against CBS-TV, NBC-TV, and ABC-TV charging
that the networks were responsible for Zamora's conviction
since he had been exposed to over 50,000 television murders.

Aggrieved plaintiffs have tried to strip television of the
most basic First Amendment guarantees. For example, no
doctrine is more sacrosanct than the prohibition of prior restraint, or prepublication censorship. Yet in a Los Angeles
courtroom last June, an NBC lawyer was cited for contempt

[3] Article by Karl E. Meyer, contributing editor. *Saturday Review.* 5:19–23.
S. 16, '78. © *Saturday Review*, 1978. All rights reserved.

—and jailed for five hours—when he refused to allow a federal judge to preview a one-hour documentary drama called "Billion-Dollar Bubble." The program, based on an actual insurance swindle, was to be broadcast that evening; one of the convicted swindlers claimed that showing the fictionalized drama might hurt his chances for parole. On that tenuous basis, the court was being asked to enjoin the broadcast. Within hours, an appeals panel of three judges voided the contempt citation, freed the lawyer, and terminated the eccentric injunction proceedings.

Consider a second example, which is not so eccentric:

Arthur Buzz Hirsch, an independent film-maker, was ordered by a United States District Court in Oklahoma to produce all documents and tapes relating to a documentary that he was preparing. Hirsch had been investigating the untimely death of Karen Silkwood, an employee in a plutonium factory owned by the Kerr-McGee Corporation in Crescent, Oklahoma, and became concerned with the adequacy of the safety precautions in the nuclear plant—certainly a legitimate subject for inquiry.

Kerr-McGee, however, apparently felt otherwise. A subpoena was served on Hirsch by the company, and the producer was ordered to divulge his notes, correspondence, and other records pertaining to the Silkwood affair. Hirsch refused, invoking the First Amendment privilege that protects journalists from revealing their confidential sources. But the district court ruled that Hirsch was in fact a film-maker, and not a newsman.

Five months later, on September 23, 1977, the ruling was reversed in a landmark decision handed down by a three-judge panel of the United States Court of Appeals for the 10th Circuit. Was Hirsch a bona fide journalist? The appellate court held that he was: "It strikes us as somewhat anomalous that the appellee would argue that he [Hirsch] is not a genuine reporter . . . implying a lack of ability, while at the same time they [Kerr-McGee] are making a major legal effort to get hold of his material. They must believe that it has promise for them in this lawsuit; otherwise, they would not be engaging in an effort of some magnitude in order to obtain Hirsch's work product."

Television reporters, producers, and network lawyers were jubilant with the *Silkwood v. Kerr-McGee* decision. It marked the first occasion in which a federal court had expressly extended the constitutional protection of sources to television. But within months, broadcasters were back on the legal barricades, contending with two formidable cases —*FCC v. Pacifica Foundation* and *Olivia Niemi v. NBC and Chronicle Publishing*—in which the same argument was posed: that there is substantially less freedom on the air than in a playhouse or movie theater.

At issue in the *Pacifica* case was a comparatively straightforward question: Does the Federal Communications Commission have the right to prohibit the use of "offensive" words on radio broadcasts? In a 5 to 4 decision, the United States Supreme Court ruled in July that the First Amendment notwithstanding, the FCC can indeed censure and punish counter-culture stations that dare to broadcast the "seven dirty words."

The *Niemi* case is in every way more complex, so much so that it has been in the courts for four years, and may remain so through 1979. What is nominally an $11 million negligence suit against the National Broadcasting Company is in reality an argument over the power of television to influence human behavior. A San Francisco jury was to decide whether a phantom rape on television produced a real-life assault, but the law suit was dismissed on August 8, when a superior court judge ruled that it was necessary to prove that NBC intended viewers to imitate the sexual attack portrayed on film. Once again, the case is on appeal and like arguments will continue.

Some facts are inarguable. On Tuesday, September 10, 1974, NBC broadcast a two-hour movie for television called "Born Innocent," starring Linda Blair. Fully aware that the film might offend some viewers, the network inserted this advisory legend at the beginning:

"Born Innocent" deals in a realistic and forthright manner with the confinement of juvenile offenders and its effect on their lives and personalities. We suggest you consider whether the program should be viewed by young people or others in your family who might be disturbed by it.

Blair—who was famous at the time for her role in "The Exorcist"—played a runaway adolescent who had been committed by her parents to a detention center. She was then "initiated" into the center's way of life by a gang-rape in a communal shower. What happened to Blair was accurately described in an *amicus curiae* brief filed on behalf of the plaintiff by the California Medical Association:

Suddenly, the water stops and a look of fear comes onto her face. Four adolescent girls are standing across the shower room. One is carrying a plumber's helper, waving it subtly by her hips. The older girls tell Ms. Blair to get out of the shower. She steps out fearfully. Then the four girls violently attack the younger girl, wrestling her to the floor. She is shown naked from the waist up, struggling, as the older girls force her legs apart. Then, the girl with the plumber's helper is shown making intense thrusting motions with the handle of the plunger until one of the four says, "that's enough."

Immediately following the broadcast, hundreds of letters, most of them angry protests, flooded into NBC offices. To be sure, a minority of viewers, many of them professionals involved in the treatment of juvenile offenders, praised the show as a serious dramatization of a national problem. It should be noted, however, that in subsequent repeats, the rape scene in "Born Innocent" was abridged.

A second inarguable fact is that four days after the broadcast, a violent scuffle occurred on a beach near San Francisco, and before it was over, a nine-year-old girl had been sexually assaulted with a beer bottle. The victim, Olivia Niemi, was white; her four assailants, then 9, 12, 13, and 15 years old, were black. Scuffles with racial overtones had hardly been unknown at Baker's Beach. But the simulated rape of a young girl by other youngsters had few, if any, parallels in local criminal records.

Had the attackers been imitating the sexual assault in

"Born Innocent"? Did they even see, or talk about, the NBC
film? Here agreement on facts ceases. Olivia's mother,
Valeria Pope Niemi, a divorcee and a committed feminist,
thought that there was sufficient evidence that television had
influenced the four youngsters, so she employed a lawyer to
bring suit against the National Broadcasting Company.

Mrs. Niemi's choice of a lawyer—70-year-old Marvin
Lewis, a rumpled Bay Area reincarnation of Clarence Dar-
row—was bad news for NBC. Lewis has become a legend
for his artistry in persuading juries to award large sums in
esoteric cases; in one memorable lawsuit, he obtained
$50,000 in damages for a woman who maintained that a
cable car mishap had changed her into a nymphomaniac.
Lewis's specialty is negligence law and, as he sees it, the
"Born Innocent" broadcast was a classic case of wanton
negligence: "There's a difference between negligence and
simply making a mistake. Negligence involves a reckless disregard for the rights of others. If, for example, I drive at 90
miles an hour down the wrong side of the road, and an acci-
dent results, my behavior is grossly negligent, and I should
be made to pay punitive damages."

Lewis argues that NBC was in effect speeding recklessly
on a one-way street. In broadcasting the rape scene in "Born
Innocent," he maintains, it ignored its own production
codes and the industry codes set by the National Association
of Broadcasters, both of which proscribe graphic depictions
of violence. In addition, NBC ignored hundreds of studies
showing the effect of television violence on youthful viewers—especially when those depicted on film are peer models,
not adults. Lewis notes that "Born Innocent" was insistently
promoted with teasers, and that it was shown at 8 P.M., a
time when youngsters were bound to be watching. Lewis
cites this quotation from a speech given on October 23, 1974,
by Charles Duffey, president of ABC: "The race for audience ratings too often blinds us to our basic responsibilities.
. . . Yes, a program like "Born Innocent" should be shown.
But no, it should not be shown at such an early hour when
children more often than not control the dial."

When Mrs. Niemi initially filed suit, NBC rejoined by opposing a jury trial of the negligence charge. At one point, in what must be regarded as an excess of zeal, NBC contended that Mrs. Niemi was unfit to hold parental custody because she was exposing her daughter to adverse publicity.

As Mrs. Niemi persisted in her refusal to consider any settlement and as adverse briefs (including that of the California Medical Association) began to accumulate, NBC turned to a New York attorney, Floyd Abrams, who many colleagues consider to be the country's foremost authority on the First Amendment. Abrams has in the past decade successfully opposed every variety of gag order on the press, most notably in the Pentagon papers case.

What Lewis sees as a simple negligence case, Abrams views as a fundamental argument over First Amendment safeguards for free expression. If *Niemi* establishes a precedent for broadcaster liability for any crime that can be remotely linked with a dramatic production—as the soft-spoken Abrams argues—then the way is open for a flood of lawsuits, of which the $25 million dollar Zamora claim is simply a foretaste.

An *amicus curiae* brief supporting NBC and prepared for the Writers Guild of America West, Inc., a screenwriters' union, puts the matter forthrightly:

This is *not* a case where the writer or publisher has uttered false facts, libeled, or invaded the privacy of a plaintiff, or advocated immediate or even remote action. The question presented, in the guild's view, is whether the writer or producer can be exposed to civil liability because, allegedly, a viewer of the drama is inspired thereby to commit a crime.

We believe there can be only one answer. In a free society writers and all others in the creative process—including actors, directors, producers, and their employers—cannot have any threat or worry of such liability. Otherwise, the First Amendment and society's right to the creativity of its members and to the reception of literary and artistic works would be crippled.

However eloquent, such lofty language cuts little ice with Marvin Lewis. As he rmarks, "They all talk about the 'chilling' effect a favorable verdict in *Niemi* would have on creators. I prefer to talk about the 'heating' effect that "Born Innocent" had on kids. Yes, it's true, there might be a flood of lawsuits against television—but it was because there was such a flood of lawsuits against automobile companies that we now have seat belts in our cars."

Nevertheless, lawsuits or the threat of them do have a chilling effect on creative expression, and can be used to restrict free speech. Faced with the probability of litigation, network programmers can be counted on to devise entertainment so devoid of ideas or controversy that by comparison "I Love Lucy" would seem risqué. Many writers and producers would concede that NBC erred egregiously in its presentation of "Born Innocent," but at the same time they fear—with reason—that emotions aroused by the case may disastrously retard the very kind of quality programming that protesting viewers insist that they want.

The writer's dilemma concerning violence on television was perceptively described by Frank Price, president of Universal TV: "Somehow it's a battle that is difficult to get stirred up about. Who, after all, is likely to proclaim himself pro-violence? The groups that would normally resist pressure tactics leading to censorship are silent on this one. Does the ACLU want to join on the side of violence?"

Few television creators would deny that the medium poses unique problems because of its "pervasiveness," the telltale word used by the Supreme Court majority in the *Pacifica* case to distinguish broadcasting from print. Recently, precisely this point was being discussed among four veteran television writers in Hollywood. David Rintels, a former president of the Writers Guild of America West, spoke for his colleagues: "I believe that 99 percent of the writers I know would agree that they should not have total, unqualified freedom to put what they want on television, and most of them would feel that writers for television should not have the final say on what appears on the screen."

Who should have the final say? The networks and sponsors, whose paramount concerns are ratings and profits?

Government regulators? Citizen groups employing boycott threats? It may well be true, in the words of Fred W. Friendly, a pioneer newscaster, that "the most serious threat to television and its claim to First Amendment freedoms is not the FCC or the Supreme Court or an imperial Presidency, but the runaway television rating process."

OUR ALL-TOO-TIMID PRESS [4]

The First Amendment does not say anything about "responsibility." This observation, which I have offered to hundreds of disbelieving and usually disapproving audiences, invariably brings some challenger to his or her feet with something like the following inquiry (usually varied more in its degree of choler than in wording): "Do you mean to say that the press has a right to be irresponsible?"

I mean to say nothing of the sort, although it's true—just to be argumentative—that irresponsibility does not appear to the layman's eye to be a constitutional violation. But it's just as well for journalists in particular to recall the skeptical judgment in *The Federalist* of Alexander Hamilton—who opposed as unnecessary a Bill of Rights for the Constitution:

What is the liberty of the press? Who can give it any definition which would not leave the utmost latitude for evasion? I hold it to be impracticable; and from this I infer that its security, whatever fine declarations may be inserted in any constitution respecting it, must altogether depend on public opinion, and on the general spirit of the people and of the government.

Just so. And with that in mind, no journalist should advocate to the public the idea that the press has "a right to be irresponsible"; no one could agree to that. Nor should any journalist wish the press or broadcast news to *be* irresponsible. Aside from their pride in their craft and its insti-

[4] Article by Tom Wicker, New York *Times* columnist, from his forthcoming book, *On Press. Saturday Review.* 5:22–3. Mr. 4, '78. © Saturday Review, 1978. All rights reserved.

tutions, their desire to do their personal work well, and their concern that the public should be informed, all journalists know that popular contempt for and fear of press irresponsibility are as grave threats—and more justified ones —to a free press as are government attempts to silence it. And, as Hamilton foresaw, that part of the First Amendment might not long survive a hostile, determined public opinion.

Granting all that, a certain case for tolerance of irresponsibility still has to be made. That is to say if the American press is to remain free—even in the somewhat limited sense that necessarily results from the conflict of this freedom with the other equally guaranteed freedoms in the Constitution and the Bill of Rights—it cannot have responsibility imposed on it by legislation, judicial interpretation, or any other process.

Freedom contains within itself the possibility of irresponsibility. No man is truly free who is not permitted occasionally to be irresponsible; nor is any institution. Responsibility, it goes without saying, is profoundly important; and the highest freedom of all may well be the freedom to conduct one's life and affairs responsibly—but by one's own standards of responsibility. It's a mean freedom in which a mere failure of responsibility brings a jail term or a fine or some other societally imposed penalty—and no freedom at all if standards of responsibility are uniform, designed to prevent rather than to punish failures, and set by some higher authority.

Yet some of the most sweeping restrictions on the freedom of the press have been proposed in the name of preventing press irresponsibility. What is lost sight of is that if responsibility can be imposed, freedom must be lost; and of those who advocate various means of ensuring the responsibility of a supposedly free press, two questions should be asked:

Who defines responsibility? In numerous instances, the difficulty editors and reporters have in determining a responsible course in disputed circumstances has, I believe, been demonstrated—notably in the case of the New York *Times*'s treatment of the Bay of Pigs story. In literally thousands of other instances—most of them less important but many on the same level of seriousness—editors have no hard-and-fast rules to follow, save those of experience, ethics, and common sense—all of which vary from person to person. Editors may, and often do, differ on what is responsible—even as *Times* editors differed among themselves on handling the Bay of Pigs story. There simply is no certainty, in most instances, as to what constitutes a responsible course in an enormous number of cases that editors and reporters have to face.

Most journalists believe that the multiplicity of editorial decisions likely to result in any given case is a major safeguard against irresponsibility and misinformation. All editors won't make the same decision based on the same set of facts—a story played on page one by the *Times* may be printed inside the Washington *Post*; a quotation in the one story may not appear in the other; different lines of interpretation may well be taken by the two papers and by any number of others, with the result that the same story appears in many versions and with a greater or lesser degree of prominence. This rich diversity not only works against the possibility that any story can be covered up or manufactured but it also offers a reasonable guarantee that differing viewpoints on the same events will reach the public.

Not only, therefore, would the imposition of standards of responsibility on the press move it away from diversity and toward uniformity of presentation but it would require an instrument big enough and comprehensive enough to define responsibility in an immense number of instances, for a huge number of publications and broadcasters. No such instrument exists, save the government.

Who enforces responsibility? This is a simpler problem. Once responsibility is defined, obviously nothing of sufficient power and scope exists to force the defined responsibility on the entire press—again save the government.

Thus, if we are to be *sure* of a responsible press, the only way is through a government that both defines and enforces responsibility. Not just Richard Nixon would have leaped at *that* opportunity. It need scarcely even be pointed out that in such circumstances, the condition of the American press would be a far cry from freedom.

Would that matter?

Obviously, a totally government-controlled press would make much difference to liberty in America; but that is not what most of those who demand greater press responsibility have in mind. They more often set forth a supposedly middle course—yielding a little freedom in a beneficial trade-off to gain some responsibility.

The middle-course argument is respectable. It cannot be maintained by the most ardent First Amendment advocate that democracy is not reasonably healthy in Britain, where the press is under much greater restraint than it is in the United States. Libel laws that sharply restrict publication and broadcasting; a heavy bias toward privacy rather than publication in laws governing press reports on criminal justice proceedings and other actions of the courts; the Official Secrets Act that governments of both parties frequently invoke, apparently not always in matters of indisputable national security; and the quasi-governmental Press Council to monitor and criticize press activities—have these stifled the larger British democracy? From my side of the Atlantic, I cannot say that they have.

For whatever reasons, the history of British politics is by no means as marked by venality and corruption as is that of the United States, and governing ethics and traditions there appear so settled that serious violations of them—for example, a power grab such as that represented by the Watergate complex of offenses—are far less likely. Secrecy by the British government has been widely accepted for centuries. Profound policy miscalculations—the Suez War, for example—bring quick political retribution, Official Secrets Act or no, while more egregious American blunders in Vietnam and Cambodia for years produced in the United States mostly a "rally-round-the-President" effect, until the press—

primarily television—finally turned the public against the war (by printing and broadcasting *news*, not editorials).

Therefore, press restraints perhaps amenable to British democracy—although not many British journalists really consider them so—would not necessarily be fitting in the United States. Should a Watergate occur in the United Kingdom, colleagues in the British press say, the governing party plausibly accused of conniving in the burglary of opposition party headquarters and then of obstructing justice to conceal the crime would soon be turned out of office, despite restrictions on reporting such a story. But it was a challenging American press that kept Watergate in the public eye and ultimately forced the various actions that led to Richard Nixon's resignation—at that, two years after the offense.

But the existence of restrictions on the British press, together with the evident survival of the essential British democracy, leads many serious and reasonable persons to suggest not government control of the American press but similar instruments of responsibility in this country's journalistic practice.

When the Senate in 1977 established an oversight committee for the so-called intelligence community, for example, one of the committee's first studies was of the need, if any, for a limited form of Official Secrets Act in the United States —an effort to protect the CIA from the public rather than the public from the CIA that stood the committee's supposed responsibility on its head.

The discussed act's reach would ostensibly have been limited to barring disclosures of "sources and methods" of gathering intelligence—"ostensibly" because although "sources and methods" describes an arcane art and is a term therefore supposedly capable of being strictly defined and narrowly applied, both the FBI and the CIA have in the past shown themselves capable of slipping large abuses through tiny loopholes. It was, for example, supposedly to protect sources and methods that some of the CIA's mail-opening and surveillance operations were illegally pursued.

Whatever the situation in Britain, in this country—as I hope I have demonstrated—secrecy has too often been used to shield blunders, crimes, and ineptitude. Alert citizens should not accept without sharp questioning a secrecy law designed to give a secret agency even greater powers of covering up its operations than it already has. And unless Congress were to show an uncharacteristic willingness to include a "shield" provision for reporters—which it has never done in other legislation of less importance and which would be of dubious constitutionality—a likely consequence would be about as follows:

The leak of a secret protected by the act would appear as a news story in a newspaper or on a broadcast. An inquiry would be launched; but as usual, the identity of the leaker (who could be prosecuted under the new law) would not be learned. The reporter-recipient of the leak would be subpoenaed to appear before a grand jury and would be asked the identity of his source, with a view to prosecuting the leaker. It would be made clear that no other means existed of obtaining this information vital to enforcement of the Official Secrets Act and the orderly administration of government.

The reporter would abide by his professional code of ethics and would refuse to answer. He would then be held in contempt and ordered to jail—although there might be no evidence of any damage to national security as a consequence of his or her story. A lot of reporters would have a lot of second thoughts—chilling indeed—about accepting leaks of so-called security secrets under such a threat.

Would that serve the cause of responsibility? Once again, the answer depends upon who defines responsibility in any given case; but those who place a high value upon a "robust and uninhibited press" and who have learned to be skeptical of the government's assertions of "national security" are not likely to think so.

But even if no such drastic step as instituting an Official Secrets Act was taken, why not more restrictive libel and

ward and Bernstein on the one hand and by the Pentagon
Papers on the other do not usually understand that such
remarkable efforts as these—whether or not they are viewed
as necessary or excessive—are limited exceptions to long-
established practice.

Undoubtedly, in the more than a decade since Dwight
Eisenhower roused the Goldwaterites with his attack on
"sensation-seeking columnists," the press has become more
activist and challenging, particularly in covering politics
and government—though *not* business and financial institutions. On the evidence of press performance in that decade
—the disclosure of duplicity and ineptitude in Vietnam; the
exposure of political corruption in the Nixon administration; the demonstration of grave threats to American liberty
by the "Imperial Presidency," the FBI, the CIA, and other
security agencies—I assert the necessity to encourage the de-
veloping tendency of the press to shake off the encumbrance
of a falsely objective journalism and to take an adversary
position toward the most powerful institutions of American
life.

By "adversary position," I don't mean a necessarily hostile position; I use the word in the lawyer's sense of cross-
examining, testing, challenging, the merits of a case in the
course of a trial. Such an adversary is opposed only in the
sense that he or she demands that a case be made: the law
stated, the facts proven, the assumptions and conclusions
justified, the procedure squared with common sense and
good practice. An adversary press would hold truth—unat-
tainable and frequently plural as it is—as its highest value
and knowledge as its first responsibility.

Such a press should be encouraged in its independence,
not investigated—even by its friends—when it asserts that
independence. A relatively toothless News Council that
nevertheless could summon editors and reporters, notes and
documents, film and outtakes, in order to determine publicly
whether editorial decisions had been properly made *by the
News Council's standards* would be bound to have an ulti-

mately inhibiting effect on editors, publishers, and broad-casters—not all of whom would therefore be dismayed. Most, it's safe to say, would rather be praised for someone else's idea of responsibility than risk being questioned or criticized for their own independence.

Somewhat similarly, tighter libel and privacy laws would surely narrow the area open to editorial judgment—and some editors and publishers might welcome such laws just for that reason. Some might even yearn privately for an Official Secrets Act because its proscriptions would relieve them of having to decide such difficult questions as whether or not to publish so-called national security stories and of the loud accusations of irresponsibility that inevitably follow such decisions, no matter how they are made.

My belief is that the gravest threat to freedom of the press is not necessarily from public animosity or mistrust, legislative action or court decision. Certainly, even though absolute press freedom may sometimes have to accommodate itself to other high constitutional values, the repeal or modification of the First Amendment seems unlikely. At least as great a threat, I believe, comes from the press itself—in its longing for a respectable place in the established political and economic order, in its fear of the reaction that boldness and independence will always evoke. Self-censorship silences as effectively as a government decree, and we have seen it far more often.

In the harsh sunlight of a robust freedom, after all, nothing stands more starkly exposed than the necessity to decide and to accept the responsibility for decision. If the true freedom of the press is to decide for itself what to publish and when to publish it, the true responsibility of the press must be to assert that freedom.

But my life in journalism has persuaded me that the press too often tries to guard its freedom by shirking its responsibility and that this leads to default on both. What the press in America needs is less inhibition, not more restraint.

A SECRETIVE SECURITY [5]

Fourteen years ago, in discussing the power and structure of America's intelligence agencies, I suggested that there can be no meaningful consent of the governed—the principle on which democracy rests—when the governed do not know to what they are consenting.

Nothing that has happened in the ensuing years leads me to believe that these thoughts were wrong, or that the situation has changed very much. Indeed, disclosures in the past few years about the abuses in the intelligence agencies, including the Central Intelligence Agency, the Federal Bureau of Investigation, and the National Security Agency, have tended to bring the point home rather dramatically. Most of the examples of official lawbreaking which have now been documented by congressional committees, by Anthony Lewis, by official inquiries of various kinds, and which are beginning to lead to some reform, were kept from us by secrecy labels. One of my favorite examples is a C.I.A. program known as Sub-Project Number 3. This was a ten-year program that was part of the C.I.A.'s broader program of behavioral control and mind control, involving, among other things, drug testing. Sub-Project Number 3 worked as follows:

On Bedford Street in Greenwich Village, New York, and on Chestnut Street on Telegraph Hill in San Francisco, C.I.A. agents secretly rented what were known as "safe houses," or apartments. These were maintained in order to experiment with drugs on unsuspecting or, as the intelligence community likes to call them, "unwitting" persons. Men were lured to these "safe houses" by prostitutes. There they were drugged with LSD, their conversations were tape-

[5] Article entitled "A Secretive Security; National Security and the First Amendment; Questions and Answers," by David Wise, lecturer, political writer, and author of *The American Police State* and *The Politics of Lying*. *Center Magazine*. p 8–16. Jl./Ag. '78. Reprinted by permission of the *Center Magazine*, a publication of the Center for the Study of Democratic Institutions, Santa Barbara, CA.

recorded, and their actions were observed through one-way mirror windows. The principal agent in charge of the San Francisco operation kept a pitcher of chilled martinis in the refrigerator, which he presumably drank as he made his scientific observations, all at the taxpayers' expense.

Of course, this was a shocking abuse of the constitutional rights of American citizens. It is also an offensive thing for our government to do. That went on for about ten years. All of the documents in this project were labeled "secret" or "top secret." Many have now been released and are in the public domain.

We could go on with horror stories of this kind. The point is, there is a conflict in our society between First Amendment values and the values we associate with national defense and national security. If we grant the premise —and I do grant it—that some types of information must be kept secret by the government, at least for a limited time, then important questions arise. Who shall decide what information shall be kept secret: the executive branch of government? the Congress? the courts? the press? What criteria should be used to define the information to be kept secret? Who shall define national security? Can national security be defined?

Perhaps even more important questions arise once secret information has escaped the control of the government. Should there be prior restraint of the press in some circumstances? Should there be prior restraint in circumstances involving "national security"? Should there be subsequent punishment of newspapers, magazines, or reporters who publish information that had been secret? Should the espionage laws be applied to journalists?

Should there be criminal or administrative sanctions applied to officials who leak secret information? Here we get into a difficult area. Do sanctions against reporters, or their sources, abridge the First Amendment or raise First Amendment questions? It would be gratifying if we could settle these questions. I don't think we can. I am not even sure there are answers to some of these questions.

The abuses of what we call our classification system, our system of official secrecy, are well-known by now. The House Subcommittee on Government Information, headed by Richardson Preyer, has disclosed that in 1976 the executive branch classified 4.5 million documents. Since a document is many pages long, the subcommittee staff estimates that forty-five million pages may have been classified in 1976 alone. I have estimated that there may be one hundred million classified documents in active government files; I think that is a very conservative estimate.

The Pentagon's chief classifier has testified that the Defense Department alone has more than a million cubic feet of classified documents, the equivalent, if stacked, of 2,297 Washington Monuments. The oldest of these documents is a 1912 contingency plan, the release of which, it was felt, might jeopardize the national security.

There are examples of ludicrous overclassification. The bow and arrow was classified by the Army in World War II as a "silent, flashless weapon." The fact that monkeys were sent into outer space was classified, although they were on display in a zoo not far from where I live in Washington, with a plaque informing visitors that they had indeed been shot into outer space.

The dollar cost of classification is hard to estimate; but the Pentagon and three other departments, according to a study now six years old, spent $126 million in one year on classification and related security of classified documents.

When I first got into this subject, some years ago, I felt that classification had always been with us. I was shocked to discover that the system of formal classification began in the civilian departments of the government, outside the military, only in 1951, with Harry Truman issuing the first executive order. Essentially that classification system has been maintained, with modifications, ever since.

President Jimmy Carter asked his staff to revise the Nixon classification order issued in 1972 and still in effect when Carter took office. From the initial draft, it appears that the reform of the secrecy system under Mr. Carter will be no reform at all. This draft would continue, with some changes, the system we have had since 1951, or at least since 1953. Enough loopholes and exemptions have been written into the Nixon order and into the first draft of the Carter order so that the government may keep secret anything it wishes to keep secret, simply by saying a document is essential to national security.

The Watergate affair gave us dozens of new examples of how classification and secrecy were used to conceal not information that was pertinent to national security, but information that was politically embarrassing, information that contained evidence of crimes committed by the highest officials of our government. Indeed, one would have thought that Watergate would have weakened the inclination of the public to support a concept of national security which has led to all these abuses. It has not had that result.

Reforms are coming along through the executive branch and through the Senate Intelligence Committee. But as far as the issue of secrecy per se is concerned, we may be heading in a direction that concerns me. There is increased talk in Washington about a legislative solution to this problem. The idea is that, since the executive branch has failed to open up information in a meaningful way, and since it will always abuse its authority to keep information secret, it is hopeless to expect self-reform by the executive branch. Therefore, the Congress, as part of a general reassertion of its authority, particularly its war power authority, must move into this area and legislate.

I think that there are great dangers in the legislative approach. I can foresee sanctions—either initially or subsequently—following such legislation. There would be an attempt to set standards of secrecy and to provide penalties for violating those standards.

This is an interesting situation. Many of the people who are opposed to secrecy and who normally might be expected to favor disclosing more information are also some of the same people—like Richardson Preyer, Morton Halperin, and others—who are now thinking and talking and writing about a legislative substitute for the executive order. That idea is tempting, but I think it might lead us in a very dangerous direction.

If sanctions do follow such legislation, or are included in such legislation, I can foresee a situation in which a future Neil Sheehan, or Anthony Lewis, or Seymour Hersh, having been given a package of important government documents dealing with a matter of public policy, such as the Vietnam war, might feel constrained to clear it with some congressional body or with a board of censors or a review commission, which has been a feature of such suggested legislation. Even if protections are written into the legislation, making it clear that no newspaper would have to abide by the decisions of such a board, there might nevertheless be great pressure on journalists to go to this official agency and decide whether one's newspaper could or should print this information.

Also, almost certainly there would be administrative, if not criminal, sanctions included such as those Admiral Stansfield Turner, the director of the C.I.A., has called for. Almost certainly administrative sanctions would be applied to officials who leak information to the press, sources on which the press depends. If such sanctions were formalized in law, you are immediately into the area of whistle-blowing —with all the implications of punishing officials who leak information about corruption, or about important policy issues that have been wrongfully kept secret from the public.

I would like to close with a quotation from Justice Hugo Black: "The press was to serve the governed, not the governors. . . . The press was protected so that it can bare the secrets of government and inform the people."

Harry S. Ashmore (Center Associate): I take it you want to confine our discussion principally to the classified information system relating to matters of national security, rather than get into other areas where confidentiality and nondisclosure are legitimately a part of government operations.

Wise: Yes.

L. Geoffrey Cowan (Attorney, Center for Law in the Public Interest; Lecturer, Communications Studies Department, University of California at Los Angeles): I am not sure I agree that the lesson of Watergate has been lost on government bureaucrats or on the Carter Administration. The lesson of Watergate for most of those people was, don't get caught. I suspect that that is a lesson which some people just learned too well.

Mr. Wise has raised the question of who decides. Should it be a review board or the courts? I think review boards are dangerous. First, I hate to think who appoints a review board. Second, I think that there is a tendency for review boards to begin to identify totally with the institution which they are reviewing. It is not likely that a review board would be independent of the intelligence community. The courts, on the other hand, tend not to have a vested interest in protecting the intelligence community and they do not instinctively believe that the intelligence world is right. Judge Murray Gurfein in the Pentagon Papers case proved that as well as anyone could have. Here he was, a Nixon appointee, his first day on the Federal bench, and he made one of the best decisions that anybody made in those proceedings. I would much prefer to take my chances with a District Court judge. Courts also provide for an adversary process, which is inevitably preferable to review-board processes. Certain rights of lawyers are built into the court process, rights that would otherwise be hard to get when you are dealing with intelligence affairs.

Here is another question we should consider. In the Pentagon Papers case, had the position of the three dissenters in that case been upheld, had the Second Circuit Court of Appeals position been affirmed, the case would have gone back to the District Court for further hearings to decide whether, in fact, the injunction should go into force. I have always wondered who would have been allowed to participate in those proceedings in the District

Court. In the first place, Judge Gurfein had already proved himself to be "untrustworthy"—from the executive branch's point of view. But leaving him aside, and assuming he was a necessary evil, would any lawyers for the New York *Times* have been allowed to participate in a process in which the government and all participants were discussing the reasons why the government was fearful about the information that would be made public? The point is that, to make its case, the government would have had to release information which was itself so sensitive that it seems to me likely they would have tried to exclude the *Times'* lawyers from participating in the court process. In fact, something of that kind has already happened in certain Freedom of Information Act cases.

One of these involved the ship, Glomar Explorer. In that case, the military audit project, I believe Jack Anderson wanted to have copies of the contracts involved with the Glomar Explorer. He asked the C.I.A. for those copies. The C.I.A. said it could not respond to that request, because it was not going to admit there were any contracts. Since it was not admitting whether there were contracts, it could not allow the contracts to be seen *in camera* by a judge. It simply said that this was an improper area for exploration.

The case was argued as well as it could be in front of a very good district judge, Judge Gerhard Gesell. Judge Gesell finally came out with his decision. He called the attorney representing the military audit project and told him that he had reached a decision. The lawyer said, "What is your decision?" Judge Gesell said, "I am sorry to deny the request." The lawyer said, "When may I get a copy of your opinion? Can I send somebody down there to pick it up?" Judge Gesell said, "I'm terribly sorry, you are not going to be able to see my opinion. I have decided that this decision is going to be put in my locked vault, and you are not to see it." The lawyer said, "Well, how can I appeal your decision, if I can't see it and can't know on what it was premised?" Judge Gesell said, "You will simply have to guess, because it is based on information I had, which you can't have access to."

So, those problems do exist when you are relying on a court system, even on a court system in which theoretically lawyers have a right to participate and act as advocates. Some guidelines have been developed to the extent that there can be guidelines for participation in those cases. But the situation cannot be satisfactory, because there is always crucial information, or information which the government will claim is crucial, and they will not give the lawyers access to that, so the lawyers cannot know what they are arguing about.

I would also reinforce Mr. Wise's point that legislation can be dangerous in these matters, although much obviously depends on the legislation and on the executive order. I have been thinking about the effect of legislation on the possibility of prior restraint. I think that inevitably the government will try to go after newspapers. The first instinct of government is to go after sources; but the damnable thing is, you can't ever find the source. The story during these last few years of investigative journalism is that nobody ever finds the source. Nobody knows who gave Daniel Schorr the stuff. Nobody knows who gave Seymour Hersh the stuff. Nobody knows who was leaking all the information about the Agnew prosecution. Somehow, the information about the source never comes out, if you can't get the reporter to talk. So there is always a desire to go after the press, if only out of sheer frustration.

I would say that if there is a court position on when prior restraint could go into effect—and this would probably be true, to some extent, of subsequent punishment of the press—it is when the publication of the information creates an immediate, inevitable consequence equivalent to the imperiling of troops at sea. That is a hard test to meet. It is the test spelled out in Justice William Brennan's opinion in the Pentagon Papers case. But I think his opinion is generally believed to be what the Supreme Court accepted as its position.

However, at least three justices—Justices Byron White, Potter Stewart, and Thurgood Marshall—seem to take the position that the reason for their ruling was that they were dealing here with a request that the Court act partly in the absence of a clear executive order; but more important, in the case of Justices White and Stewart, they seem to be saying their ruling was affected by the absence of congressional legislation on classification. It is possible to read the Supreme Court's Pentagon Papers decision in a way which suggests that if the classification scheme had been established by legislation, those justices might have voted the other way; they might have agreed to the government's request that publication of that information be restrained.

Brent Rushforth (Attorney, Center for Law in the Public Interest): I approach this from a quite personal point of view. Over the last several years I have been a public interest lawyer with the Center for the Law in the Public Interest, which I helped to found in Los Angeles. Insofar as I have been involved in these kinds of issues, it has been as an advocate in court on behalf of the public's right to know. I have developed some biases that lead me to believe and conclude, as a matter of personal opinion, that our system of government functions better when the public's right to know is expanded.

Now, I will shortly be going to Washington to become an Assistant General Counsel of the Department of Defense. About a month ago, I was sitting in the Pentagon with the head of the National Security Agency, the general counsel for the Pentagon, and a fellow named Vice-Admiral Daniel Murphy, who has been brought into the Pentagon from the Navy, and who now runs their intelligence operation.

We began to discuss many issues related to these kinds of problems, one of which was proposed legislation sponsored by Senator Edward Kennedy and Senator Birch Bayh, among others. It would require the National Security Agency and other intelligence-gathering agencies like the

Defense Intelligence Agency, to go to a special seven-judge court, established by appointment by the Chief Justice of the United States, to argue for a warrant before they could go and gather intelligence from, say, the Russian Embassy. I am told—and I have no reason to disbelieve it—that our technology is such that one can gather any piece of conversation or any communication virtually anywhere.

The arguments in that discussion were that to require the National Security Agency or, for that matter, any other intelligence-gathering agency, to go through such a procedure would be virtually to preclude it from gathering the intelligence vital to the national security interests of the United States. The primary argument is that to tell anyone outside the intelligence community—albeit here we are talking about seven of presumably the most prestigious and trustworthy people in the country, judges appointed by the Chief Justice—would be a breach of security, and that this would almost insure that the Russians, or whomever we wanted to bug, would know what we were going to do before we did it.

Now, I came into the Pentagon with all these strong personal feelings, all of these biases in favor of public disclosure. But even so, there comes very quickly a strong tug, if you will, in the direction of the bureaucracy's interest and in the direction of the agency's interest, all of which, of course, is always couched in very persuasive arguments of national interest.

Ashmore: Almost everybody would agree that any kind of revelation of information that jeopardized troop movements, or people at sea, would probably be an improper, if not illegal, act. On the other hand, take the example of the Bay of Pigs. With hindsight now, most people would agree that if the New York *Times* had published what it knew, that would have aborted the Bay of Pigs operation. Certainly that would have jeopardized a number of people who were in it.

Cowan: If information on the Bay of Pigs business had been brought out, that would not have fit Justice Brennan's definition of the kind of information whose disclosure would have immediately and inevitably imperiled American troops. Disclosure of the Bay of Pigs plans would have prevented the operation, and so there would not have been people whose lives would have been endangered. The point at which the Brennan admonition would exist would be if the planes had just taken off and were in midair. At that point if a flash bulletin on the Associated Press wire service reported what kind of planes they were and where they were going—

Anthony Lewis (Columnist, the New York *Times*): I agree. Justices Stewart and Brennan, in the Pentagon Papers case, concurred not only in their short opinions, but also in what they said in the course of the argument of the case. They agreed that the revealed information would have to result in very direct and immediate causation, not political causation or something that might happen at the end of some long discussion, in order to meet their test for prior restraint of publication.

The hard case for me is not the military case, but the disclosure, say, that the Foreign Minister of Hungary—to take a hypothetical example—had been paid by the C.I.A. The causation there would be very direct. He would be shot at dawn. Would the kind of direct, immediate, irreparable, grave damage to the nation or its people—which is Justice Stewart's phrase—also go for the death of a single person? I don't know.

But I want to echo two thoughts of Geoffrey Cowan. One concerns the risk of not allowing the newspaper and its lawyers to get at the information which they need in order to argue the matter. That was a very acute reality in the Pentagon Papers case. We learned long afterward, from a book published by the US Attorney in the case, Whitney Seymour, Jr., that the reason the government declined—

even in the *in camera* hearing of the case before Judge Gurfein—to point with particularity to portions of the papers that could, as the government claimed, destroy the country, was that Seymour had been instructed by the Defense Department and others that he could not do so if anyone except the judge was present.

The reason that the case came out differently in New York and Washington—there were two branches in that case—was that in Washington, Judge Gesell waved aside the objections of the government to allowing reporters and editors of the Washington *Post* to remain in the room when they discussed the papers. He just would not have it. He said, "Oh, no, we've got to have them here. They know what it's all about. They'll tell us what's true, false, and so on." So, what followed in the proceedings was that every time either a government witness or lawyer said, "This is a dark secret, your honor. Look at this. This will cause the world to tremble," a Washington *Post* reporter covering the Pentagon or the State Department would say, "Judge, that matter was discussed before the Senate Foreign Relations Committee on June 2, 1970." This literally happened, and the case collapsed under the impact of this knowledge.

I must say I find myself both less and more optimistic than David Wise and Geoffrey Cowan. Mr. Cowan is very worried about President Carter. Yet, I note the one distinctive feature of his proposed executive order is that it is the first one in the history of the United States, as far as I know, that was handed out for comment before it was issued. That is a very big plus. I think it deserves to be noted.

Similarly, while I worry in many of the same ways that David Wise worries, I have to say that looking, in the large, at what information gets out of the government these days, I can remember no period of our history or any other country's history when information was in fact freer, when more issues of defense and foreign policy were disclosed, and leaked. If you were, say, a representative of a foreign government in the United States these last few years, you would have to assume that if you talked to a US official about

something this week, you would read it on all the wire services the next week. That doesn't always happen, but it happens to a considerable extent. And it happens without the hysterical reaction that was the usual case in the previous Administration. We can well imagine what Henry Kissinger's reaction would have been to some of the things that have been disclosed since he left government.

We are, in fact, in a much more open period than we were in the Kissinger age, when, quite apart from classification of documents, policy was made by a single person, Mr. Kissinger. Ambassadors, his own aides, even the President of the United States, did not know what Mr. Kissinger was doing, and they were not permitted to know. So, in all those respects, I am rather more optimistic.

On the other hand, I strongly share the sense of danger that both Mr. Wise and Mr. Cowan have expressed about legislation to handle this problem. Indeed, I can add two more judges to the three Geoffrey Cowan mentioned in the Pentagon Papers case for whom the absence of legislation was significant. Both Justices Black and William O. Douglas, though they said they took an absolute view of the First Amendment, spoke of the significance for them of the absence of legislation. As a matter of fact, Justice Douglas' opinion mostly dealt with that matter. So, I think it is unquestionably true that any legislation in this field, however it was said to be confined, might have a significant effect on the attitudes of judges who, for various good reasons, are less willing to act without legislative encouragement than they are with it. I very much share that concern of Mr. Wise.

I would even be against legislation that said it was exempting the press and other recipients of secrets from its aim. For example, in the Ford Administration, legislation was proposed of the kind that I suppose Admiral Turner has in mind, to protect the sources and methods of intelligence. It was drafted by the Attorney General, Edward Levi, or perhaps by the C.I.A. In any case, Mr. Levi put his imprimatur on it.

In order to avoid what they rightly thought would be the outcry from the press, which is effective in stopping legislation in this area, they said in their legislation that, though injunctions were to be authorized against the disclosure of intelligence sources and methods of a certain grave character, those injunctions were to apply only to the tellers of the secrets, not to the receivers, namely the press.

However, under questioning, the Attorney General agreed that if it became known that a newspaper possessed such secrets, e.g., the Pentagon Papers, which surely contained a good deal of material that would have been claimed to involve intelligence sources and methods, and if the government did not know from whom the newspaper had obtained this material, the government would almost certainly summon, or could summon, the editors or reporters of the newspaper before a grand jury—since, in addition to the injunctive proceeding, there was a criminal aspect to this proposed statute—and inquire of them from whom the material came. Thereafter, the government could proceed against the editors and reporters for not answering the question. I do not think it is possible to draft legislation without having some effect on the right to publish. So, I agree with David Wise that legislation is dangerous.

I think there are equal dangers under the heading of government litigation. That tends to get by with less notice from the press and public and to stir less outrage. There is pending a civil suit brought by a number of people who were surveilled—if that is a word—by the C.I.A. in the course of the C.I.A.'s domestic spying program, called Operation Chaos. These people have sued those who conducted the surveillance, Richard Helms and other former officials of the C.I.A. In the course of this suit for damages, they have sought, by discovery, the documents describing the nature and extent of the program. They got a number of documents declassified, with various passages blanked out. Thereafter, the Justice Department in Mr. Carter's Administration sought and obtained from a US District judge an order forbidding the plaintiffs or their lawyers to make these unclassified documents public. That is one of the most outrageous things that has happened in this area in quite a long time. There has been little notice of that; it is just an obscure lawsuit. But I think it is most threatening. The very purpose of the lawsuit, as in many such lawsuits, may well be to inform the public, not to enrich the plaintiffs, which, in any event, is quite unlikely.

Wise: This raises a question that I find more troublesome than sanctions against the press. There was a grand jury in Boston that investigated Neil Sheehan and his wife and others in connection with the Pentagon Papers. No indictments were brought. But I find it very easy to say that any indictment of reporters, any subsequent punishment of reporters for publishing classified material, would constitute an abridgement of the First Amendment. I don't know, however, whether the Supreme Court would agree with that position.

If reporters are prosecuted for breaking and entering, that is one thing. But if they are prosecuted for printing information, that is another. I would be opposed to the latter. When reporters cease to act as reporters and act as criminals, then I think they open themselves up to criminal prosecution. But the prosecution would then be for theft, not for what they have published.

Lewis: Such sweeping statements always worry me a little. I don't like exemptions for the press that are that total. Suppose it were not a reporter, but a professor. Suppose a professor had published something about Vietnam, and had been investigated by the same grand jury?

Wise: That is a kind of a Popkin-in-sheep's-clothing question.

Lewis: Exactly. It is a real case, the case of Professor Samuel L. Popkin, who was put in jail in November 1971, because he refused to tell the government how he came to know the existence and authorship of the Pentagon Papers.

Wise: I was thinking in more conventional terms of the press as we know it. I would not even try to begin to define the question of what is a journalist.

But the thing I have more difficulty with concerns sanctions against those who leak the information. The requirements of bureaucracy or the orderly transaction of government would seem to indicate that those who go outside channels with information might be subject to some kinds of discipline. And to say that often this is a case of whistle-blowing of such magnitude as to make the action justifiable does not reach all of the cases in which information might be passed, but was not of such a clear nature as the one involving Ernest Fitzgerald and Lockheed's C-5A program, for example.

What about the possible First Amendment impact of either legislation or just administrative action, taken against government officials who leak information, particularly in the national security area?

Cowan: I am not convinced that the First Amendment applies in the case of the people who leak information. I think there are punishments that would clearly be excessive. But I think some kind of punishments would seem to be legitimate. Obviously they would have to be tailored to the offense.

Let me give you an analogy to another leading recent Supreme Court decision having to do with gag orders, in the Nebraska Press Association case. In some ways, that is a better case than the Pentagon Papers case from the standpoint of its absolutism. Interestingly, the Burger decision says you can do nothing to prevent newspapers from printing what goes on in a courtroom, or information about a case in advance. But you can put all kinds of gags on people who might provide that information. I think that probably is the state of the law today.

As to the narrow question of whether the First Amendment should protect people who leak information, it seems to me, assuming that the restrictions are clear and suffi-

ciently narrow, and assuming that the punishment, whatever it may be, fits the crime, then the First Amendment is not violated.

Lewis: I do not agree with that. The late Alex Bickel said something with which I agree, and which I think is fundamental to our notion of these issues. It is that the government and the press are separate interests under our system. The government is entitled to do its best, and will do its best, to keep those secrets it desires to keep. And the press will do its best to get those secrets out. Each has an interest, and will fight it out. On the whole, Bickel said, it is best not to resort to law to referee that struggle. It ought to be a political struggle, not one that is adjudicated. When you adjudicate things, they tend to end up less free than they were before. Our system is disorderly, but it is our system. I agree with Bickel.

On the other hand, picture Seymour Hersh trying to find out about the Glomar Explorer, and reaching a former crewman of the Glomar Explorer, one who takes a liking to Mr. Hersh. He says to Mr. Hersh, "I'll meet you for a drink tomorrow at noon, and I'll tell you all about it." In the meantime, the government discovers this, and rushes to court to enjoin the seaman—if it could do that—from talking. I don't see that there is much difference in the First Amendment interest at that stage. It seems to me there clearly is a First Amendment interest of the crewman, as well as of Mr. Hersh, as well as of the public.

Cowan: The right of free speech under the First Amendment, apart from the right of the press, the right of free speech gives the crewman the right to speak about what he knows.

Lewis: Yes, within the same kinds of limitations as the press has. I would say that if he had not violated any statute, or the Espionage Act, and if the government could not show grave, immediate, irreparable damage, or the likeli-

hood of that to the nation or its people, then the crewman's interest in free speech must prevail. The First Amendment does include something about speech, as well as the
press.

Cowan: And you think that the crewman's superiors, who
had given him this information, with, say, the understanding that he has it in complete confidence, would be wrong
in docking him for revealing it?

Lewis: I said former crewman.

Cowan: Yes, I think it is possible that the limitations should
end with the employee's severance from the government. I
also do not see how prior restraint would get into it. I am
thinking about the kinds of reprimands that are built into
an executive order.

Lewis: There we are in agreement. That is the Bickel theory. The government can reprimand its employees; it can
do its best within its own system. I accept that. Where I
get off the train is when I leave the abstract case of the
crewman and go to the actual reality of, say, Victor Marchetti, the ex-C.I.A. employee. For the government to require, as a condition of employment, the signing of a
secrecy agreement, which it can then use, without any
standard of proof of damage to the country, to restrain Mr.
Marchetti for the rest of his life from ever saying anything
about the subjects with which he dealt while in the C.I.A.,
certainly seems to me to involve the First Amendment.

Ashmore: Doesn't this get you to a point where there is no
effective official sanction against someone who leaks unau-
thorized information? Then you don't have a classification
system that means anything.

Lewis: I am agreeing with Geoffrey Cowan. The First
Amendment does not prohibit administrative action against
present employees of the government, or of the Glomar Ex-

plorer, or whatever. I agree that the government is entitled to demand a degree of orderliness within its own ranks.

But the reality is that leakage is widespread, it is wholesale, it is accepted. Since the Kissinger era nobody really does much about it. My own notion is that leakage is such a part of the system now, and the government, when it wants to, has such weighty administrative weapons, that we don't need to change the system and give government more weapons.

Wise: Do you feel that the inclusion in the law of administrative sanctions against leakers would have any First Amendment impact, or make any difference in terms of the First Amendment, compared to the existing system of administrative sanctions contained in the executive order?

Lewis: For the reasons previously indicated, I am wary of getting into legislation. I agree with you. Who knows what implication would be drawn from it? The only thing I would say against that, and this opens up a much larger question, is that perhaps because of the inevitable bureaucratic momentum and attitude, the executive branch tends to be more protective of the principle of secrecy than today's congressional committees are. For example, the drafts of the intelligence charters that I have seen from the Senate Intelligence Committee are much better, much more complete, much fairer than the executive order just issued. So there might be a trade-off; you might benefit in one way from legislation and, at the same time, run a risk because of that legislation.

TWO THEORIES OF PRESS FREEDOM [6]

Many of the most celebrated recent First Amendment decisions of the United States Supreme Court have involved

[6] Article, entitled "Two Theories of Press Freedom Are Parallel, Yet Bound to Meet," by Floyd Abrams, New York lawyer who has represented a number of First Amendment cases, and lecturer at Yale Law School. New York *Times.* p IV, 11:1. My. 7, '78. © 1978 by The New York Times Company. Reprinted by permission.

the claim that some other constitutional right should out-
weigh the right of freedom of expression. In the Pentagon
Papers case, the Government argued that publication of
documents about the war in Vietnam would significantly
interfere with the foreign policy of the nation and with decisions entrusted by the Constitution to the President; in a
series of cases involving the effort of many trial judges to
restrict what the press may print about the courts, the claim
was made that such restrictions were necessary to enforce
the Sixth Amendment (fair trial) rights of defendants in
criminal trials. Both arguments were rejected—but in other
cases, including those involving the right of journalists to
protect their confidential sources, the press has fared less
well.

Last month, the Supreme Court decided a difficult case
in which the core question was of a different nature: not
whether a First Amendment claim triumphed over some
other constitutional claim but which of two First Amendment claims should prevail. At issue was the constitutionality of a Massachusetts statute which made it a crime for
banks and business corporations to spend money to influence the vote on referendums. The law forbade such companies to mount a publicity campaign for or against laws
unless the laws "materially affected" their business.

Two banks and three companies wished to spend money
to publicize their views that the Massachusetts Constitution
should not be amended to permit a graduated personal income tax. Under the Massachusetts law, such expenditures
would plainly have been criminal. But was the law itself
constitutional?

The Supreme Court, by a 5-4 vote, decided it was not.
Associate Justice Lewis F. Powell Jr.'s opinion (for himself,
Chief Justice Burger and Justices Stewart, Blackmun and
Stevens) concluded that the speech the corporations wished
to make related directly to governmental affairs. As such, the
speech was "indispensable to decision making in a democracy" and no less so because corporations rather than individuals were the speakers.

To three other members of the Court—Justices White, Brennan and Marshall—the Powell ruling was a "drastic departure" from earlier decisions of the Court. The dissenting opinion argued that Massachusetts, in adopting its statute, had itself made a choice based upon other long-recognized First Amendment interests—those of preventing "domination of the electoral process by corporate wealth."

Perhaps the most striking aspect of the decision had nothing to do with who should win the case. In a provocative eight-page concurring opinion, Chief Justice Burger articulated views squarely at odds with views previously expressed by, among others, Justice Stewart. The issue dividing Chief Justice Burger and Justice Stewart was not the constitutionality of the Massachusetts statute; in fact, both joined in Justice Powell's opinion in favor of the corporations. What divides the two members of the Court is an issue likely to be more significant than even the result in the Massachusetts case: whether the fact that the First Amendment bars abridgements not only of "freedom of speech" but "of the press" means that the press is entitled to any First Amendment rights beyond those rights of free speech guaranteed to all citizens.

Justice Stewart's views on the subject were expressed in a speech at the Yale Law School in 1974. To Justice Stewart, the free-press guarantee of the Constitution deliberately extends special protection to the publishing business—"the only organized private business that is given explicit constitutional protection." Freedom of the press, he argued, does not just mean that newspaper publishers are permitted to speak freely, as are the rest of us; what it means is that the press was specially designated in the Constitution to be autonomous of the Government, so that it may provide "organized, expert scrutiny of government." As such, it requires special protections to preserve its independence. According to Justice Stewart, the Constitution does not require that the press be given "access to particular Government information" or "openness from the bureaucracy"; it does require that "the autonomous press may publish what it knows, and may seek to learn what it can."

Chief Justice Burger's concurring opinion in the Massachusetts case takes direct issue with the idea that the "institutional press" has any freedom beyond or different from that of the public generally. In explaining his view, which led him to conclude in this case that corporations require substantial First Amendment protection if the press itself is to be protected, the Chief Justice explained the basis for his belief that no special protection exists for the press. There is simply no historical basis, he argues, for such a conclusion. Beyond that, he contends, the very process of defining *who* might be entitled to any special protections is perilous and "is reminiscent of the abhorred licensing system of Tudor and Stuart England—a system the First Amendment was intended to ban from this country." The First Amendment, the Chief Justice concludes, "does not 'belong' to any definable category of persons or entities: it belongs to all who exercise its freedoms."

The philosophical difference between the Stewart and Burger views does not surface in every First Amendment case. In the Massachusetts case itself, as well as in a number of other First Amendment cases, Justice Stewart and Burger voted together. In fact, both have recently written vigorous defenses of press freedom from governmental intrusions. Justice Stewart's Yale speech, for example, argued that even though the press is sometimes "outrageously abusive, untruthful, arrogant and hypocritical," it "hardly follows that elimination of a strong and independent press is the way to eliminate abusiveness, untruth, arrogance, or hypocrisy from government itself." And Chief Justice Burger, in a landmark 1973 decision for the Supreme Court, had observed that even though editors "can and do abuse" their power, it remained the fact that "for better or worse, editing is what editors are for;" and that the authors of the Bill of Rights had deliberately taken "calculated risks of abuse" by editors "in order to preserve higher values"—those of freedom of expression.

Sooner or later, the Court is likely to address directly the question of whether the press requires *special* constitutional protection. Last week, the Court found it unnecessary to do so in a unanimous decision that held unconstitutional a Virginia law making it illegal for anyone to "divulge" information about secret proceedings concerning the fitness of judges. The statute, the Court held (in an opinion by Chief Justice Burger) was unconstitutional because it infringed on the rights of all who did not participate in the secret proceedings to speak freely about matters "near the core of the First Amendment." Justice Stewart filed a separate opinion arguing that the statute was unconstitutional, but urging as his reason that "if the constitutional protection of a free press means anything, it means that government cannot take it upon itself to decide what a newspaper may or not publish."

III. THE CASE OF MYRON A. FARBER

EDITOR'S INTRODUCTION

The issue of freedom of the press has already been discussed in Section II of this compilation, yet a current and related case has raised so many thorny issues that it would seem to merit a section of its own. Such is the case of M. A. Farber, a respected investigative reporter for the New York *Times*. In 1975, Mr. Farber began investigating a mysterious series of deaths that had occurred in the 1960s in a small New Jersey hospital. The deaths formed a pattern: the victims were all postoperative patients who had come through their respective surgical procedures apparently without incident; all of them died of inexplicable respiratory failure; none was a patient of a surgeon referred to in Mr. Farber's *Times* articles as "Dr. X." As a result of the Farber stories, several of the bodies were exhumed and examined by pathologists who reported finding traces of curare, a muscle-relaxant in a number of them. The curare was traced to "Dr. X," who was identified as Dr. Mario Jascalevich and charged with murder.

So far the story is a simple one with no constitutional overtones: reporter's hard investigative work gets story; authorities react to story and make arrest; suspect is charged and put on trial. That the charge is murder and the defendant's life is at stake adds, of course, immeasurably to the importance of the trial. In the course of his defense, Raymond Brown, representing Dr. Jascalevich, requested all of Mr. Farber's notes on which the articles had been based, claiming that they might prove crucial to his client's case. Both Mr. Farber and the New York *Times* declined to comply, citing the First Amendment guarantee of freedom of the press and also New Jersey's so-called Shield Law, giving news gatherers the right to refuse to disclose the sources of their information. As a result, both Mr. Farber and the New

York *Times* were found to be in contempt of court. Until each complied with the court's order for the material, Mr. Farber was to be jailed and the newspaper fined $5,000 per day. After slightly more than two weeks in jail, Mr. Farber was released pending appeal, only to be reincarcerated when the New Jersey Court of Appeals upheld the trial judge.

Then, on October 24, 1978, the jury dramatically acquitted Dr. Jascalevich. Released from their penalties for contempt of court, Mr. Farber was let out of jail and the *Times* no longer had to pay the $5,000-a-day fines that had by this time amounted to $285,000. Nevertheless, since Mr. Farber and the *Times* had already appealed the New Jersey decision to the US Supreme Court, the constitutional issue of a reporter's notes remained alive. Shortly thereafter the Supreme Court decided not to hear the appeal, which settled very little except that in the state of New Jersey, Mr. Farber and the *Times* were not constitutionally protected in respect to the Jascalevich case. Some of the articles in this section—presented in chronological order—were written amid the controversies over Farber's position well before the case had ended in acquittal.

Several interesting questions arise in the discussion of this case, including at which point does a reporter's protection under the First Amendment (freedom of the press in this instance) give ground to the defendant's protection under the Sixth Amendment (the right to a fair trial)? To just what extent does the press have the right to withhold the background material of stories it has published—particularly when a defendant's life is at stake? Are positions on the issue altered in any way by the disclosure that Mr. Farber was working on a book on the Jascalevich case and that the New York publishing firm of Doubleday had offered him a sizable advance against future royalties?

The initial selection in this section concerning Mr. Farber's situation is a summation by Deirdre Carmody of the *Times* of the issues as they were initially seen. Following this is a reasoned piece by New York *Times* columnist Anthony Lewis (who used to cover the Supreme Court), in which he points out that a separate hearing on whether Farber's notes were in fact relevant to the case might have avoided the contempt issue. The third selection, from the *New Yorker*'s "Talk of the Town" section warns of a possible chilling effect of the court's request upon freedom of thought itself. Next Haynes Johnson, a respected journalist for the Washington *Post*, disagrees with the *New Yorker* piece and worries more about the effect of the money Mr. Farber stands to make out of his book and what effect that might have on Mr. Farber in particular and journalism in general.

In the fifth selection, reprinted from the *Philadelphia Inquirer*, Bernard M. Borish, former chancellor of the Philadelphia Bar Association, states the conflict between the First and Sixth Amendments and strongly advocates, like Anthony Lewis, a judge's *in camera* inspection of the disputed material before ruling on whether it must be made available to the defense. In the sixth article, Ronald Dworkin, in the New York *Review of Books*, comments on the privileged position of reporters in relation to principle and policy as far as the First Amendment is concerned.

And finally, there is the New York *Times*'s own editorial position commenting on the doctor's acquittal and the treatment of Mr. Farber throughout the trial.

COURTS AND THE PROCESS OF NEWS GATHERING [1]

The case of M. A. Farber, the New York *Times* reporter who has been convicted of contempt of court for refusing to turn over his notes in connection with a New Jersey murder trial, is the latest in a series of court decisions around the country involving the news-gathering process. They involve the increasingly troublesome question of whether a news organization is protected by the First Amendment and state

[1] Article by Deirdre Carmody, columnist. New York *Times*. p A10. Jl. 28, '78. © by The New York Times Company. Reprinted by permission.

shield laws from turning over notes or other material amassed during the course of news gathering.

Mr. Farber is scheduled to go to jail at noon today unless the United States Supreme Court extends a stay that will allow him to go free while his case is being appealed. The *Times* and Mr. Farber have been asked by the defense counsel for Dr. Mario E. Jascalevich to turn over all notes, documents and other material relating to Mr. Farber's 1975 investigation of 13 allegedly suspicious deaths at a New Jersey hospital in the 1960s. Dr. Jascalevich is now standing trial for five of the deaths.

Mr. Farber has been fined $2,000 and sentenced to go to jail until he turns over the material. He faces an additional six-month jail sentence for criminal contempt, to be served separately. The New York *Times* has been fined $100,000 plus an additional $5,000 for each day the material is not turned over.

There have been about 40 contempt orders against reporters in the last six years resulting in more than a dozen actual jailings that lasted from just hours to weeks. The reporters are saying that they are protected by the First Amendment from turning over material. The plaintiffs in these cases generally hold that there are overriding concerns, such as a person's right to a fair trial or the right of a person suing for libel to have access to material that will prove him right.

What are the courts saying?

The Background

The United States Supreme Court has said that while a reporter who has witnessed a crime must testify before grand juries the same as anyone else, the First Amendment does accord some protection to the news-gathering process. "Without some protection for seeking out the news, freedom of the press could be eviscerated," Associate Justice Byron White wrote in *Branzburg v. Hayes* in 1972.

In that same opinion, however, he went on to say, "From

the beginning of our country, the press has operated without constitutional protection for press informants and the press has flourished. The existing constitutional rules have not been a serious obstacle to either the development or retention of confidential news sources by the press."

The Branzburg case still stands as the major Supreme Court ruling on the subject of confidential sources. Twenty-six states now have reporter shield laws, which give reporters the privilege of refusing to disclose in legal proceedings any information obtained in the course of news gathering. But judges have consistently found ways to get around these shield laws. In the Farber case, Judge William J. Arnold, the presiding judge in the Jascalevich trial in Superior Court in Hackensack, N.J., has said that he will not consider the New Jersey Shield Law (one of the strongest in the country) until after he examines the material himself *in camera*. The *Times* and Mr. Farber are arguing that the shield law protects them from turning over the material not only to the defense attorney, who requested it, but to the judge, too.

When the New York *Times* and Mr. Farber went to Justice White earlier this month asking him, in effect, to quash the subpoenas against them, he refused to do so, stating, "There is no present authority in this Court that a newsman need not produce documents material to the prosecution or defense of a criminal case."

The Press's View

The press generally takes the position that if a newspaper reporter is forced to turn over material gathered in the course of an investigation, the very functioning of a free press will begin to wither. This reasoning is based on the belief that the framers of the Constitution meant the press to be a kind of overseer of government that would be free to report not on what the government said it was doing but on what the government was actually doing. In order to do this, the press has to depend on informants within the government, and to be able to assure these informants that their identities will not be made public. The best example of this is probably the reporting on the Watergate scandal, where the real workings of the government were able to be revealed to the public because informants within the government trusted reporters not to disclose their identities.

The basic assumption of the American press is, therefore, that the First Amendment guarantees not only the right to print but the right to gather information.

There is also the belief that the framers of the Constitution made it quite clear that the press was to be separate from the government. If the courts, acting at the request of either prosecutor or defense, can examine and make public all the files, all the unpublished notes, all the unassessed raw material that a reporter has gathered, the press becomes nothing more than an instrument of the courts.

There is also the belief that the editing process itself is protected by the First Amendment and that raw notes should not be seen by anyone. A reporter in the course of his news-gathering writes down many things that are said to him that, upon investigation, may turn out to be totally untrue. They may also appear to mean one thing out of context when in actuality they mean something entirely different. Most editors and reporters agree that this potentially damaging material should be free from all scrutiny.

Finally, again given the view of the framers of the Constitution, the press should not become an investigative arm of government. News organizations should not have to help out in investigations that law enforcement authorities with all the tools at their disposal can conduct themselves. Mr. Farber has argued that whatever he uncovered in his investigation of the deaths in New Jersey is similarly available to the defense.

The Opposing View

There are many lawyers who argue that while the First Amendment does indeed protect the press in many ways, there are times when it should bow to other overriding concerns. The most dramatic example is when a person is on trial for his life, like Dr. Jascalevich in the Farber case.

Under the Sixth Amendment, he has a right to a fair trial and nothing should prevent him from the free exercise of that right. The right to life, in this view, supersedes the more speculative assertion of news organizations that the free press will be damaged if a reporter or a news organization is made to turn over reporters' notes and other materials.

Ironically, a defendant on trial for, say, shoplifting, has exactly the same constitutional rights to a fair trial as a defendant in a murder case. It could become a rather sensitive balancing act to find the exact spot when a particular amendment becomes more overriding than another.

But the strongest belief is that we have a system of laws, and when a court has spoken after hearing both sides, that court must be obeyed. If a reporter is ordered to turn over material by a judge, then, this view holds, the reporter is putting himself above the law by refusing to comply. It is tantamount to saying that the press is an elitist group that can flout the law when it disagrees with it. It is also, in effect, saying that the First Amendment is more important than others and that it must always prevail.

The Outlook

Most press lawyers feel that there is a patchwork of decisions being handed down in courts across the country at this point about just what a reporter's rights are under the First Amendment and state shield laws not to turn over material. They feel that the United States Supreme Court will at some time take one of these cases and that when it does, its views will constitute a major press decision.

THE FARBER CASE [2]

The jailing of M. A. Farber, the New York *Times* reporter who refused to submit his notes to a New Jersey judge, is one of those hard cases that seem destined to make

[2] Article by Anthony Lewis, author and Pulitzer prize-winning national reporter. New York *Times.* p A17. Ag. 7, '78. © by The New York Times Company. Reprinted by permission.

bad law. Freedom of the press, respect for the courts, the public interest: All are likely to suffer.

When the press and the courts clash—and that is happening more and more often—the press sometimes sounds as though its constitutional position must always prevail. I think there are important values on both sides. Whenever possible, therefore, confrontation should be avoided. What makes the Farber case so unfortunate is that this confrontation was unnecessary.

Mr. Farber uncovered suspicious circumstances in a series of hospital deaths years ago. As a result a doctor, Mario E. Jascalevich, was charged with murder. At his trial his lawyers asked to see all of Mr. Farber's notes of interviews. The judge ordered them submitted to him, so he could look at them in private and decide whether they should be made available to the defense. When Mr. Farber and the *Times* refused, he sent the reporter to jail and fined the paper $5,000 a day to force compliance.

A defendant charged with a serious crime may have good reason to see the notes of a reporter who stirred up the case against him. For one thing, not all reporters are as responsible as Myron Farber, nor all papers as respected as the *Times*.

Suppose that, during the McCarthy period in the 1950s, a red-baiting magazine ran an article charging some man with illegal Communist activity. The man is tried. His lawyers have reason to think that the witnesses against him, in talking to the writer for the magazine, made statements inconsistent with what they are now saying on the stand. Shouldn't the lawyers be able to probe those inconsistencies?

One of the great libertarian decisions of the Warren Court, *Jencks v. U.S.*, held that those prosecuted by the Federal Government must be able to check the prior statements of Government witnesses for inconsistencies. Soon after the decision, in 1957, Congress wrote that principle into a statute, providing that sensitive material go to a judge first for his private scrutiny.

Against that interest of a defendant the press asserts its

interest in keeping the government out of its business—particularly when the names of confidential sources may be disclosed. That is a powerful interest. But under our law, even strong claims do not usually result in an absolute privilege against being required to produce important evidence.

The Nixon case is the decisive example. A President's private conversations would ordinarily be regarded as immune from forced disclosure. Indeed, in the tapes case, the Supreme Court said they were covered by a constitutionally based privilege. But the privilege was not absolute. It was overridden, the Court held, by the particular needs of law enforcement.

Those are the kinds of claims that might have to be balanced in an ultimate resolution of the Farber case. But they did not have to be resolved now, and the confrontation might have been avoided altogether. That is clear from an aspect of the case that not everyone has noticed.

In asking for the reporter's notes, defense counsel made no showing of why particular things might be useful. They asked for everything. And the only reason they gave for needing it was an unsupported charge that Mr. Farber had conspired to "concoct" the murder charges. Their subpoena had the ring of the sort of fishing expedition that wise judges refuse to allow.

Here again the Nixon case is illuminating. Archibald Cox, the first special prosecutor, gave specific reasons for wanting to hear particular conversations the very first time he asked for any tapes. Leon Jaworski did the same. And the foundation they laid was crucial to the Supreme Court decision.

Mr. Farber and the *Times* argue that a judge, before calling for a reporter's notes, should require at least a preliminary showing that they are likely to be relevant material and necessary. That seems a restrained and reasonable rule. If it had been imposed in this case, Dr. Jascalevich's counsel might have been unable to meet it—and the confrontation avoided.

New Jersey's higher courts may still be wise enough to

rescue the trial judge from his mistake and require such a showing. If that happens, and if the defense then can meet the test, I think the reporter and the paper will face a compelling obligation to comply—especially if they are asked only to let the judge read the particular notes in private.

Submission of highly sensitive matters to judges *in camera* is standard procedure. The system works well, without violation of confidences.

Some in the press have said loosely that a judge is just another arm of the state, to be resisted, but that is the opposite of the truth in this country. Our courts are independent enough to stand up to a President. It would be a grave mistake for the press, if it has a fair hearing, to put itself above the law.

NOTES AND COMMENT [3]

The subpoenas served on the *Times* and its reporter Myron Farber at the request of the defense in the murder trial of Dr. Mario E. Jascalevich require them to turn over to the court all notes and memos written in connection with Farber's articles on the case. There is wide agreement among reporters that the subpoenas, if they survive appeal, will set a legal precedent that will seriously damage reporters' ability to gather news. They contend that sources who wish to remain anonymous will simply cease to speak once it becomes clear that reporters can be forced to disclose their informants' names in court. These sources, it is pointed out, would no more want to confide in such reporters than they would want to confess their sins to priests who were obliged to pass on to the local police station everything they had been told. Even from the standpoint of law enforcement, the results will be ironic, because reporters who can be compelled to identify their sources in court aren't going to learn anything that the courts want to know. As soon as the courts start fishing for evidence in this pond, the pond will dry up.

[3] Notes and Comment. *New Yorker.* 54:23. Ag. 14, '78. Reprinted by permission; © 1978 The New Yorker Magazine, Inc.

The courts will then lose not only any confidential information that the reporters may have possessed but also the articles based on that information—articles that on many occasions in the past have brought the very existence of crimes to the government's attention in the first place. Thus, at a single stroke the judicial system will defeat both the First Amendment and itself.

These dangers seem to us reason enough to reject the subpoenas, but there are other dangerous consequences, which are also worth consideration. They concern not freedom of speech but freedom of thought. Freedom of speech is guaranteed by the Constitution and freedom of thought is unmentioned there, but in practice the two freedoms belong together. The *Times* subpoena calls for notes that were made in preparation for the writing of articles. Notes of this kind are usually nothing but aids to memory, and, as such, are auxiliary to thought. You might call them a sort of thinking on paper. Like most thoughts, they are tentative, provisional, experimental. They may even be unfounded, wild, irresponsible. Inside the mind, a freedom reigns that is less confined than any speech—a freedom amounting, in fact, to license. This reckless, unbridled quality of thought seems to be desirable in the production of even the most sober writings. But the thoughts themselves—and the notes that reflect them—were never meant for presentation to the world. Even when they are notes of conversations with others, they are indiscriminately inclusive, and may contain much that is trivial, gossipy, malicious, inaccurate, or actually untrue. Another kind of notes—for first drafts and the like—may contain false starts, wrong guesses, and foolish or worthless notions of every kind. In short, a writer's notes contain precisely everything that he and his newspaper have *rejected* for publication. In groping behind published works for information, the Government does more than cause writers the embarrassment of seeing their unpolished drafts dragged before the public; it lays hands on a writer's thoughts. If prior restraint (prevention of publication) has a chilling effect on free speech, then obligatory disclosure of notes (enforcement of publication) has a chilling effect on free thought. For although the licentious profusion of words and ideas that shows up in a writer's notes is unworthy of public exposure, it is essential to the work that precedes publication. It can be said of some of these notes that they are the record of a writer's interview with himself. It may be here—in the solitude of the mind—that freedom really begins. In these silent exchanges, a writer becomes his own source. And this source, more than any other, perhaps, requires confidentiality, and without confidentiality will refuse to tell the world what it knows.

FARBER CASE DULLS THE EDGE OF THE PRESS' SILVER SWORD [4]

Two weeks ago Myron Farber, a reporter for the New York *Times*, surrendered himself to authorities at the Bergen County Jail in Hackensack, N.J. "I'm not going to jail because I want to go to jail," he told reporters as he walked into prison. "What I'm trying to do is uphold the Constitution of the United States. I'm going to jail for what I believe to be the public interest."

Nothing guarantees wider news coverage than the jailing of a reporter in a freedom-of-the-press case, and Farber's certainly has been no exception. He has been seen on national television standing in his cell while the prison doors clanked shut. The network talk shows and the newspaper columns have been filled with impassioned defenses of his actions.

Farber has become the latest of the press cause célèbres, a journalist fighting for all those things journalists cherish— the peoples' right to know, the protection of a reporter's confidential sources, the resistance of government intrusion into the gathering of news and publishing process. The Con-

[4] Article by Haynes Johnson, editor, author, and Pulitzer Prize-winning national reporter. Washington *Post*. p A3. Ag. 16, '78. Reprinted by permission.

stitution means exactly what it says, and the First Amendment stands supreme: thus, the arguments and the press case repeatedly made for him.

All terribly noble-sounding, all embracing the highest principles of a free press. And, suddenly, now all not so simple, and not as things first appeared.

The Farber case has taken a turn that, at the least, brings embarrassment if not dismay to the press. Far from being the detached, independent reporter of legend, operating without self-interest and motivated only by a search for the truth, Myron Farber has been shown to have a large stake in this case. He stands to profit handsomely from it. The more publicity, the greater the potential financial return. That old, uncomfortable question about money and the media—and how each affects the rights of individuals in a criminal trial —has arisen again.

No press freedom principle has been debated more vigorously in recent years than that of protecting news sources. As the struggle between media and Government has intensified in the post-Vietnam/Watergate era, and the inevitable constitutional conflicts between guaranteeing a free press and a free trial have become more complicated . . . the vital role of the press in investigating wrongdoing in public news sources has assumed paramount importance.

Without an assurance of confidentiality in critical cases affecting the public interest, it's claimed again and again, news sources would "dry up." Citizens whose careers—or even their lives—could be in jeopardy if their names were revealed as sources, properly would be reluctant to give information to the press.

Many news organizations and numerous journalists (including this one) have made these arguments in court cases over the last several years; and have submitted sworn affidavits to buttress their views.

At first blush the Farber case seemed destined to become a classic in this regard. Here was a reporter whose painstaking investigations had resulted in the opening of a criminal case and the subsequent murder indictment. Dr. Mario E.

Jascalevich was indicted after a series of articles by Farber in the *Times* suggested that a "Dr. X" had murdered patients at a small Jersey hospital by injecting them with a paralyzing drug, curare. Jascalevich is now on trial in that murder case; there would have been none had it not been for Farber's reporting, and for the *Times* publishing what he found.

The doctor's defense lawyer served subpoenas on Farber and the *Times*, requiring them to turn over all the reporter's notes, records and memoranda in connection with the case. After the trial judge ordered Farber and his paper to comply, they refused. Freedom of the press and the First Amendment: they were going to protect their confidential news sources, even if it meant Farber's going to jail and the paper paying a heavy financial penalty for a contempt of court citation.

In addition to the customary arguments about the need to maintain confidentiality of sources and threats to press freedom, an intriguing new one had been made in this case. The *New Yorker* magazine argues the Farber case concerns not only freedom of the press, but freedom of *thought*. Farber's notes made in preparation of his articles are really extensions of his thoughts in this view.

"In groping behind published works for information," the *New Yorker* says, "the government does more than cause writers the embarrassment of seeing their unpublished drafts dragged before the public; it lays hands on a writer's thoughts. If prior restraint (prevention of publication) has a chilling effort on free speech, then obligatory disclosure of notes (enforcement of publication) has a chilling effect on free thought."

That's a provocative argument, and well worth pondering in future—but it now bears no relevance on the Farber case.

It turns out that Myron Farber tried to sell a book on the "Dr. X" case to Doubleday, but the proposal was rejected. Once Dr. Jascalevich was indicted, however, Doubleday then gave Farber a contract. Farber received a $75,000 advance.

He has been working on the manuscript, has turned over some seven chapters to his book editor, and there are possibilities of a movie deal in the works.

When Farber appeared in court to present his latest petition for release from jail, the judge sharply questioned him about his book. While he was refusing to provide his notes on the case to the defense lawyers, he was "profiting handsomely" from the murder trial through his book, the judge said. He also suggested that Farber had a financial stake in seeing the doctor convicted. "He has it in his power, perhaps . . . even to obtain an acquittal for Jascalevich," the judge said. "Yet, ironically, if he obtains an acquittal for Jascalevich, the book goes down the drain."

You don't have to accept the judge's reasoning to concede that all those high-sounding statements about journalistic integrity and courageously protecting news sources in defense of the Constitution now appear compromised. It's OK to sell the material to a publishing house, but not to turn it over to a defendant in a murder trial.

Myron Farber has a right to his manuscript. He has a right to refuse disclosing his sources. He has a right, even, to be wrong. But he does not, in this corner anyway, have a right to claim special moral privileges in this particular case.

What he's done, wittingly or otherwise, is lend credence to the belief he's not only interested in protecting his news sources—he's also protecting his financial interests. That perception affects more than Farber and the *Times*; it concerns the entire press.

THE FARBER CASE IS NOT A BLACK AND WHITE ISSUE [5]

The Farber case has caused much hand wringing among the nation's press, with frequent proclamations of the imminent demise of the First Amendment. Regrettably, instead

[5] Article by Bernard M. Borish, lawyer and former Chancellor of the Philadelphia Bar Association. Philadelphia *Inquirer*. p 9A. Ag. 17, '78. Reprinted by permission of The Philadelphia Inquirer, August 17, 1978.

of informing the people about the difficult issues in the case, the headlines and news commentary have berated "an imperial judiciary" and inveighed against "judicial fiat." Such inflammatory statements are neither accurate nor helpful to an understanding of the problems passed by the fair-trial/free press conflict. For the people truly to know, what is needed is not purple prose but a fair and informative analysis of the facts and the difficult legal issues.

The Bill of Rights contains "Ten Pillars of Freedom," but many citizens have only a vague idea what these rights are. At the outset, therefore, it should be made clear precisely which interests are involved and what is the nature of the conflicting interests. Constitutional rights are not absolute. Constitutional problems involve questions of reasonableness, proximity and degree in light of the particular facts of particular cases. A delicate balance must be made whenever there is a conflict, and different interests are given different weights in making the balance.

The First Amendment guarantees not only freedom of religion, the right to assemble peaceably and the right to petition for redress of grievances, but provides also that "Congress shall make no law . . . abridging the freedom of the press." The latter is the press interest involved in Farber.

The Sixth Amendment relates to procedures that the government must follow when it seeks to bring its vast powers to bear against any person to deprive him of life, liberty, or property. In the same mandatory language as the First Amendment, the Sixth provides that in all criminal prosecutions the accused shall have the right not only to a speedy public trial by an impartial jury, to be informed of the nature of the accusation, to be confronted with the witnesses against him, and to have the assistance of counsel, but also "to have compulsory process for obtaining witnesses in his favor." The experience of centuries has demonstrated the value of these procedures to one on trial for crime.

In the Farber case the defendant is accused of murder, the most serious of crimes. He has asserted that Farber and the New York City pathologist and the state's chief witness collaborated with the state's prosecutor to concoct charges of murder against an innocent citizen for pecuniary gain and to advance their careers. Pursuant to the Sixth Amendment (and a similar right granted in the New Jersey Constitution) the defendant subpoenaed certain documents admittedly in the possession of Farber and the New York *Times* for an *in camera* inspection by the trial court.

Because the trial is in New Jersey and Farber was in New York, it became necessary to employ a statutory procedure to secure Farber's attendance in the New Jersey criminal proceeding. The defendant filed petitions on two different occasions and the trial judge, who had sat through some 22 weeks of criminal trial, certified that the documents sought "are necessary and material" and that "substantial constitutional rights of . . . (the defendant) to a fair trial, compulsory process and due process of law are in jeopardy without the appearance of Myron Farber and documents so that an *in camera* examination can be made."

When Farber and the New York *Times* refused to obey the subpoena, they were held in civil contempt. Farber was committed to jail until he complied with the subpoena, and the New York *Times* was fined for its noncompliance with the subpoena. On this record, the Supreme Court of New Jersey and two justices of the Supreme Court of the United States have refused a stay of the trial judge's order.

From the trial judge's vantage point, suppose for one moment that there is a basis in fact for the defendant's allegations. Suppose there is information among Farber's documents which might contain or lead to evidence that could exculpate the defendant. Surely the press would not then advocate that Farber should be permitted to suppress that evidence on a claim of privilege. While the press obviously has a great and proper interest in protecting confidential sources, an accused on trial for murder has an equally compelling interest in having relevant evidence produced. That is the delicate balance confronting the trial judge.

Reporters and prosecutors are people, just like the rest

of us. Some of them have been known to have feet of clay, just like the rest of us. They, like us, do not always act responsibly. It is not all that long ago that a reporter took as a lover a powerful politician while covering his political activities. There are documented cases of prosecutors who have acted with less than honorable motives to advance political careers. Just this last Friday, it came out that Farber has contracted with a publishing firm to write a book about the case and took a $75,000 advance. The defense now argues that Farber's real interest is in book sale profits rather than his privilege as a reporter.

What is a trial judge to do, therefore? The New Jersey Shield Law grants a privilege, but it is not self-executing in disputed cases. In Farber there is a serious dispute and the narrow issues are who shall determine and how it shall be determined whether the disputed claim of privilege shall be sustained or denied. In our Government of laws, it can only be and must be the trial judge. It cannot be an interested person, whether the President of the United States, the New York *Times*, a reporter or anyone else.

This problem occurs all the time in courts. Litigants claim privilege for allegedly super-sensitive, top-secret information. To rule intelligently, the trial judge requests production for a private inspection *in camera*. Such an inspection is standard procedure and has worked well, preserving the confidentiality of the information and making it available, when relevant, under suitable protective court orders.

James Madison, the father of the Constitution, once described the Bill of Rights as a paper barrier against the power of the community, intended to control the majority from those acts to which they might otherwise be inclined. Madison said that the true guardians of these rights against encroachment were independent tribunals of justice.

The bulwark of our liberty is a free and independent judiciary. Democratic self-government cannot endure without a free and independent judiciary respected alike by press and citizens.

THE RIGHTS OF MYRON FARBER [6]

Dr. Mario Jascalevich . . . [was] on trial in New Jersey, charged with the murder, by curare poisoning, of a number of hospital patients in 1965 and 1966. His indictment was the direct result of a series of articles about the deaths of these patients written by a reporter for the New York *Times*, Myron Farber. Jascalevich's lawyer, Raymond Brown, asked the trial judge to order Farber and the *Times* to turn over to the defense all the notes, memoranda, interview records, and other material Farber compiled during his investigation. Judge Arnold ordered, instead, that all such material be delivered to him, so that he himself could determine whether any of it was sufficiently relevant that it should be given to Brown. Farber refused this order, and was jailed for contempt, though he has since been released. The *Times* at first refused to deliver any material in its control, and was also cited for contempt, and forced to pay large daily fines. It has since handed over certain files, but the judge who imposed the fines, Judge Trautwein, charges that these files have been "sanitized," and do not cure the contempt.

Farber and the *Times* appealed to the New Jersey Supreme Court (whose decision against their appeal was announced just as this issue of the New York *Review* went to press). They claim that Judge Arnold's order was illegal on two different grounds. They argue that the order violated the New Jersey "Shield Law," which provides that in any legal proceeding a newsman "has a privilege to refuse to disclose" any "source" or "news or information obtained in the course of pursuing his professional activity." They also argue that, quite apart from the Shield Law, the order violated their rights under the First Amendment to the US Constitution, which provides for "freedom of the press."

Each of these legal arguments is controversial. It is argu-

[6] Article by Ronald Dworkin, professor of jurisprudence at Oxford and Fellow at University College, lecturer at New York University Law School, and author of *Taking Rights Seriously*. New York *Review of Books.* p 36-8. O. 26, '78. Reprinted with permission from the *New York Review of Books.* Copyright © 1978 Nyrev, Inc.

able that the Shield Law, in so far as it grants newsmen a privilege not to disclose information which might tend to prove an accused criminal innocent, is unconstitutional because it denies the accused a right to a fair trial guaranteed by the Sixth Amendment. If so, then Judge Arnold acted properly in asking that Farber's notes and material be furnished to him privately so that he could determine whether any of them might tend to support Dr. Jascalevich's innocence.

The First Amendment argument is weaker still. The Supreme Court in a 1972 decision, *Branzburg v. Hayes*, denied that the First Amendment automatically grants newsmen a privilege to withhold sources and other information in legal proceedings. Four of the five majority justices stated categorically that newsmen have no special privilege under the First Amendment beyond those of ordinary citizens. Mr. Justice Powell agreed that the reporters in the cases the Court was considering did not have the privileges they asserted. But he added, in a short and cryptic concurring opinion, that in some circumstances the First Amendment might require courts to protect newsmen from disclosure orders which serve no "legitimate need of law enforcement." He spoke of the need to strike "a proper balance between freedom of the press and the obligation of all citizens to give relevant testimony with respect to criminal conduct."

I do not interpret Powell's opinion as recognizing a First Amendment privilege against disclosure ordered at the request of a criminal defendant, which is a very different matter from disclosure requested by the prosecution or other law enforcement agencies. State courts have disagreed about the correct interpretation of Powell's opinion, however, and some have recognized a newsman's privilege to withhold information requested by the defense when it appears that that information would be at best only tangentially relevant to the defense's case. But even if this interpretation of Powell's opinion is correct, Judge Arnold acted properly in ordering the material furnished to him privately, so that he could determine its relevance and importance to the defense, and the extent to which "freedom of the press" would be compromised by its public disclosure.

So it is at least doubtful that the legal arguments on which Farber and the *Times* rely are sound. The affair has been debated publicly, however, not as a technical legal issue but as an event raising important questions of political principle. Commentators say that the dispute is a conflict between two fundamental political rights, each of which is protected by the Constitution. Farber and the *Times* (supported by many other newspapers and reporters) appeal to the right of free speech and publication; they say that this right, crucial in a democracy, is violated when the press is subjected to orders that impede its ability to gather information.

Those who support Judge Arnold argue that the right of free speech and publication, though of fundamental importance, is not absolute, and must sometimes yield to competing rights. They therefore appeal to the principle, which they take to be paramount, that a criminal defendant has a right to a fair trial, which right, they say, includes the right to use any material that he might reasonably think supports his innocence. Both sides share the assumption that in these circumstances one or both of two important civil rights must be compromised to some degree, though they disagree where the compromise should be struck.

But the assumption they share is wrong. The privilege claimed by Farber has nothing to do with the political right to speak or publish free from censorship or constraint. No official has ordered him not to investigate or publish what he wants, or threatened him with jail for what he did publish. Judge Arnold's subpoena is very different from the government's attempts to stop the New York *Times* from publishing the Pentagon Papers or from the prosecution of Daniel Ellsberg or even the civil actions against Frank Snepp. It is, no doubt, valuable to the public that reporters have access to confidential information. But this is not a matter of anyone's right. The question raised by the Farber case is not the difficult question of how to compromise competing rights, but the different question of how much the efficiency of reporters, valued by the public, must nevertheless be sacrificed in order to ensure that Dr. Jascalevich's right to a fair trial is not compromised at all.

The public argument over the Farber case fails to notice an important distinction between two kinds of arguments that are used to justify a legal rule or some other political decision. Justifications of *principle* argue that a particular rule is necessary in order to protect an individual right that some person (or perhaps group) has against other people, or against the society or government as a whole. Antidiscrimination laws, like the laws that prohibit prejudice in employment or housing, can be justified on arguments of principle: individuals do have a right not to suffer in the distribution of such important resources because others have contempt for their race.

Justifications of *policy*, on the other hand, argue that a particular rule is desirable because that rule will work in the general interest, that is, for the benefit of the society as a whole. Government subsidies to certain farmers, for example, may be justified, not on the ground that these farmers have any right to special treatment, because it is thought that giving subsidies to them will improve the economic welfare of the community as a whole. Of course, a particular rule may be justified by both sorts of arguments. It may be true, for example, both that the very poor have a right to free medical treatment and that providing treatment for them will work for the general interest because it will provide a healthier labor force.

But the distinction is nevertheless of great importance, because sometimes principle and policy argue in opposite directions, and when they do (unless the considerations of policy are of dramatic importance, so that the community will suffer a catastrophe if they are ignored) policy must yield to principle. It is widely thought, for example, that crime would decrease, trials be less expensive, and the community better off as a whole if strict rules of criminal procedure that guard against the conviction of the innocent, at the inevitable cost of some acquittal of the guilty, were abandoned. But that is an argument of policy against these procedural rules, and so it would not justify relaxing the rules if those who are accused of crime have a right (as most liberals think they do) to the protection the rules provide.

The distinction between principle and policy is relevant to *Farber*, because the arguments Farber and the *Times* make, in defense of a special newsman's privilege to withhold information, are arguments of policy not principle. I do not mean that classical First Amendment arguments are arguments of policy; on the contrary the core of the First Amendment is a matter of principle. Individual citizens have a right to express themselves free from government censorship; no official may limit the content of what they say, even if that official believes he has good policy reasons for doing so, and even if he is right. Many Americans thought that it was in the national interest to censor those who opposed the war in Vietnam. No doubt it was in the interest of the community of Skokie that the American Nazi Party be forbidden to march through that town. But as a matter of principle the war protesters had a right to speak and the Nazis a right to march, protected by the Constitution, and the courts so decided.

Reporters, columnists, newscasters, authors, and novelists, of course, have the same right of free expression as other citizens, in spite of the great power of the press. Peter Zenger, the colonial publisher with whom Farber is sometimes compared, was jailed because he attacked the governor in print, and it was the object of the press clause of the First Amendment to prohibit that form of censorship. But newsmen do not, as a matter of principle, have any greater right of free speech than anyone else.

There are, however, reasons of policy that may justify special rules enhancing the ability of newsmen to investigate. If reporters' confidential sources are protected from disclosure, more people who fear exposure will talk to them, and the public may benefit. There is a particular need for confidentiality, for example, and a special public interest in hearing what informers may say, when the informer is an official reporting on corruption or official misconduct, or when the information is information about a crime.

This is the argument of policy that justifies the Shield Laws many states have enacted, like the New Jersey law described earlier, and that justifies a variety of other special privileges newsmen enjoy. The Justice Department has adopted guidelines, for example, instructing its agents not to seek confidential information from reporters unless the information is crucial and unavailable from other sources. The special position of the press is justified, not because reporters have special rights, but because it is thought that the community as a whole will benefit from their special treatment, just as wheat farmers might be given a subsidy, not because they are entitled to it, but because the community will benefit from that.

The *Times*'s own arguments confirm that the privilege it seeks is a matter of policy not principle. It argues that important sources will "dry up" if Judge Arnold's order is upheld. It is hard to evaluate that argument, though it does not seem powerful, even as an argument of policy. The Supreme Court's decision in *Branzburg* v. *Hayes*, though its full force is debatable, plainly held that a reporter may be forced to reveal his sources when that information would be crucial to a defendant's case, as determined by a trial judge. So even now reporters cannot, or should not, flatly promise an informer confidentiality. Any such promise must be qualified, if the reporter is scrupulous, by the statement that under certain circumstances, not entirely defined by previous court decisions, and impossible to predict in advance, a court may legally compel disclosure.

Judge Arnold's order in the Farber case—that he be allowed to review a reporter's notes to determine whether any material there would be important to the defendant's case even though the defense has not demonstrated the probability of such material—arguably extends the *Branzburg* limitations on confidentiality. But it is unclear how much the extension, if any, increases the risk that public disclosure

will in the end be made, and unclear whether there are
many informers not already deterred by *Branzburg* who
would be deterred by the additional risk of disclosure to a
judge alone. It is therefore entirely speculative how far the
general welfare would suffer if the information that might
be provided by informers of that special sort were lost.

In any event, however, this argument of policy, however
strong or weak as an argument of policy, must yield to the
defendant's genuine rights to a fair trial, even at some cost
to the general welfare. It provides no more reason for overriding these rights than the policy argument in favor of
convicting more guilty criminals provides for overriding the
rights of those who might be innocent. In both cases, there
is no question of competing rights, but only the question
of whether the community will pay the cost, in public con-
venience or welfare, that respect for individual rights requires. The rhetoric of the popular debate over *Farber*,
which supposes that the press has the rights that must be
"balanced" against the defendant's rights, is profoundly
misleading.

It is also dangerous because this rhetoric confuses the
special privileges newspapers seek, justified on grounds of
policy, with genuine First Amendment rights. Even if this
special privilege has some constitutional standing (as the
four dissenting justices in *Branzburg* suggest), it has been
and will continue to be sharply limited to protect a variety
of other principles and policies. It would be unfortunate
if these inevitable limitations were understood to signal a
diminished concern for rights of free speech generally. They
might then be taken as precedents for genuine limitations
on that fundamental right—precedents, for example, for
censorship of political statements on grounds of security.

It is both safer and more accurate to describe the privilege of confidentiality the press claims not as part of a
constitutional right to freedom of expression or publication
but as a privilege frankly grounded in efficiency, like the
privilege the FBI claims not to name its informers, or the
executive privilege Nixon claimed not to turn over his tapes.

In *Rovario* v. *US*, the Supreme Court held that neither the FBI nor its informers have any right (even a *prima facie* right) to secrecy, although it conceded that, for reasons of policy, it would be wise for courts not to demand disclosure in the absence of some positive showing that the information would be important to the defense.

A president's executive privilege is, as the Court emphasized in the *Nixon* case, not a matter of his right, or the right of the government as a whole. It is a privilege conferred for reasons of policy, in order that the executive may function efficiently, and it must therefore yield when there is reason to believe that a different public interest—the public's interest in guarding against executive crime—demands constraint on the privilege. If the strong policy arguments in favor of executive privilege must yield when that privilege would jeopardize the prosecution of a crime, then *a fortiori* a newsman's privilege, supported by weaker policy arguments, must yield when it opposes a defendant's right to gather material that might prove him innocent.

So the question raised by *Farber* is simply the question of how far the defendant's moral and constitutional right to information extends, not simply against newsmen, but against anyone who has the information he wants. Several shrewd commentators, who do not dispute that the newsman's privilege must give way if the information in question is vital to the defense, nevertheless argue that Judge Arnold's order was wrong in this case because Brown, the defense lawyer, had not shown any reasonable prospect that Farber's notes were important to his case. They point out that it would be intolerable if every criminal defendant was able to subpoena all the notes and files of any newspaper which had reported on his case, in the thin hope that something unexpected might turn up. Lawyers call that sort of investigation a "fishing expedition"; and courts have always refused defendants an opportunity to fish in anyone's files.

Indeed, it has been suggested that Brown made his request not because he believed he would discover anything useful to his client but because he hoped that the request would be refused, so that he could later claim, on appeal, that the trial was unfair. (It has also been suggested that Judge Arnold ordered the material requested to be shown to him privately, instead of rejecting the request outright, to frustrate this supposed strategy.) It would have been better (these commentators suggest) for the judge to require some initial showing by the defense why it was reasonable to suppose that the files would contain relevant material, before ordering the files to be shown to him alone.

Even this more moderate position seems wrong on the facts of this particular case, however. Farber's investigations were responsible for the police reopening a murder case years after their own investigation had been suspended. He accumulated a great deal of information not previously available, and it is not disputed that this information was the proximate cause of the indictment. In particular, Farber discovered and interviewed witnesses who now appear to be vital to the prosecution and who might have made statements to him that either amplified or contradicted their testimony or the accounts he published. There is, of course, no suggestion here that Farber has deliberately withheld anything that would be helpful to the defense. But he, like any other reporter, exercised editorial judgment, and he should not, in any case, be expected to be sensitive to the same details that would interest a good lawyer whose client is on trial for murder.

These facts are sufficient to distinguish the present case from imagined cases in which the newspaper has done not much more than report on facts or proceedings developed or initiated by others. Judge Arnold held that Farber's unusual role in the case in itself *constituted* a showing of sufficient likelihood that his files contain material a competent defense lawyer should see; sufficient at least to justify the judge's own preliminary examination of the file. Perhaps he would have required a further showing of probable relevance, or a more precise statement of the material sought, if the trial were not a trial for murder. Perhaps another judge would have required some further precision even in a murder case. No doubt Judge Arnold should have held a hearing at which lawyers for Farber and the *Times* could have put their legal objections and asked for greater specificity before they were found in contempt. (The New Jersey Supreme Court has now held that in the future such a hearing must be held if requested.) Nevertheless Judge Arnold's decision, that the facts of this case in themselves constitute the necessary demonstration, shows commendable sensitivity to the problems of a defendant faced with an investigation whose very secrecy deprives him of the knowledge he needs to show his need to know.

But it was not, I should add, reasonable to order Farber to jail or to order the *Times* to pay punitive daily fines while their legal arguments were pending before appellate courts. They relied in good faith on their understanding of the Shield Law and the First Amendment. Federal Judge Lacey, in a hearing on Farber's petition for habeas corpus, emphasized that Farber had undertaken to write a book about the Jascalevich case. Many newspapers and columnists have since assumed that the proposed book weakens Farber's case either legally or morally. It seems to me, on the contrary, almost irrelevant. Farber's contract with his publisher does not make the book's publication conditional on the conviction of Jascalevich, and there is no shred of evidence either that Farber will publish in the book material that he sought to withhold from the court or that he has any financial or personal stake in Jascalevich's conviction. There is no reason to doubt that Farber would have acted just as he did even if he had not planned to write a book. It is useless to say that they should have complied with Judge Arnold's order, and contested its legality later. They believed that their rights would have been violated, and the principles at stake compromised, even by an initial compliance with the judge's order. They were wrong, but our legal system often gains when people who believe that law and principle are on their side choose not to comply with orders they believe illegal, at least until appellate courts have had a chance to consider their arguments fully, and it served no purpose to jail

Farber or fine the *Times* before their arguments were heard. Certainly it was not necessary to defend the dignity of Judge Arnold's court or of the criminal process. If Farber and the *Times* make immediate appeal to the US Supreme Court, the New Jersey Supreme Court, even though it has upheld Judge Arnold's decision, should stay execution of further fines, and of its order that Farber return to jail, pending an expeditious ruling on that appeal.

The courts must at all costs secure Dr. Jascalevich's right to a fair trial. But within that limit they should show, not outrage, but courtesy and even gratitude to people like Myron Farber who act at personal sacrifice to provide the constant judicial review of principle that is the Constitution's last protection.

THE DOCTOR AND THE PRESS [7]

When the *Times* fell silent last August 9, our colleague M. A. Farber had just gone to jail for refusing to show his notes about a New Jersey murder case to a judge at the trial of Dr. Mario Jascalevich. That most curious criminal case has since ended in a most curious fashion. The doctor, after enduring a 34-week trial and many years of strain on his professional reputation, was acquitted on all counts by a jury that in the opinion of trial observers reached a proper verdict. And as the case ended on October 24, so did the punishment of the New York *Times* and Mr. Farber, whose stories two years ago had revived interest in some mysterious deaths a decade earlier. But our criminal convictions stand. Mr. Farber spent nearly six weeks in jail and the *Times* paid fines totaling $285,000 for both civil and criminal contempt of court.

So while the murder case is over, the case of the constitutional rights—and needs—of the press has been left in disarray.

[7] Editorial from the New York *Times.* p A26. N. 9, '78. © by The New York Times Company. Reprinted by permission.

Mr. Farber's notes were sought to prove collusion between the reporter and the prosecution and thus to impugn some testimony against the doctor. The notes were refused, even for private inspection by the judge, because we contend that the Constitution's First Amendment, guaranteeing freedom of the press, implies the right of reporters to protect the confidentiality of their source. We maintain that a right to print the news carries with it a right to gather news and that without confidentiality the sources of much valuable information would soon dry up.

The Supreme Court has never defined such a constitutional privilege for the press but it did invite Congress and the states to provide it by law, as New Jersey did. Moreover, as many as five Supreme Court justices have commented in a relevant case that invading a newspaper's files does indeed invade its First Amendment rights; in fact they speculated, in nonbinding opinions, how such invasions ought to be restrained. Thus there was and remains a basis for the *Times*'s claim, in this and other cases. It is the claim—and the plea—that confidential materials should be demanded of us only when they are absolutely necessary and relevant to a judicial proceeding and when they cannot be obtained from other, less sensitive sources.

In this sense, there may sometimes exist a conflict between the First Amendment rights of the press and the Sixth Amendment rights of a defendant. Such collisions are best avoided altogether. When they occur, the courts generally—and wisely—insist on the most rigorous procedures before one right is made to yield to another. Mr. Farber and the *Times*, however, have not had the benefit of any protective procedures; indeed, we never had a hearing at which to dispute or narrow the court's demand for *all* our files. For persisting in our claim, Mr. Farber and the *Times* have suffered penalties that already represent a considerable threat to the news media, few of which can afford such fines and legal fees.

The normal way to balance competing rights is through

judicial hearing. In a belated and confused intervention, the New Jersey Supreme Court decided last month that a hearing to justify the invasion of newspaper files is indeed necessary—in all cases save ours. Mr. Farber had waived his right to a hearing by his "intransigence," the majority decided, speculating that a hearing would only result in the same order that he had already chosen to defy.

Until the final day of the trial, when a further six-month sentence on Mr. Farber was suspended, judges up and down the system showed unusual animus toward him for what they deemed to be the arrogance of the press. And they showed almost no sensitivity to the damage that their handling of his case was doing to the business of news gathering. The *Times*'s petition for review is still before the United States Supreme Court. We are left to hope that even if the Court chooses now to let lie the conflict between the First and Sixth Amendments, it will at least rise to the defense of the Fifth, which holds that no person should be deprived of life, liberty or property without due process of law.

IV. FREEDOM OF ASSEMBLY IN SKOKIE, ILLINOIS

EDITOR'S INTRODUCTION

"No man is an island," wrote the seventeenth century poet and divine John Donne in a famous "Devotion," adding that "Any man's death diminishes me, because I am involved with Mankind," and ending with the immortal—if chilling—words: "Never send to know for whom the bell tolls. It tolls for thee." Civil libertarians might amend Donne's remarks to read "any man's loss of liberty diminishes mine." Other students of constitutional law clearly disagree. In any event, the battle of the meaning of the First Amendment's guarantee of the right to assemble has been joined over a particularly divisive—and as yet unresolved—issue.

The right to assemble covers all sorts of occasions, from Saint Patrick's Day parades through outdoor concerts to political rallies in public parks. But what happens when a group considered noxious by an undoubted majority of the nation's populace expresses a desire to parade through an area whose inhabitants have a special reason to find them particularly loathsome? Such was the situation when the American Nazi organization, the National Socialist Party, adulating Adolf Hitler and all he stood for, announced its desire to hold a rally in a Chicago park. The park was quickly declared off limits for such purposes and the Nazis then declared they would, instead, hold a march through the streets of the Chicago suburb of Skokie. They could hardly have made a more inflammatory decision—which was, of course, their intention. Skokie is inhabited primarily by Jews, a large percentage of whom are survivors of the Nazi Holocaust. Here indeed was an issue to test the mettle of the most dedicated civil libertarian!

Historically, the institution most zealous in its efforts to safeguard constitutional rights has been the American

Civil Liberties Union (ACLU). Historically, too, the ACLU
has had a large percentage of Jewish members—witness perhaps to the proposition that those who have known perse-
cution are among the first to rally against it. Obviously the
Nazi/Skokie situation presented the organization with a
cruel dilemma. In the end, the ACLU defended the Nazis'
right to march. As it turned out, the Nazis were allowed to
hold their rally in two small Chicago parks and consequently
called off—or postponed—their Skokie march, but the constitutional question remains vividly alive.

The opening article by Carl Cohen, reprinted from
the *Nation*, argues that even those who are offensive have
rights under the Constitution. The author, a distinguished
professor of philosophy at the University of Michigan, has
served both as chairman of the Michigan affiliate of the
ACLU and member of its national board of directors. The
second selection, "Marching Through Skokie" written by
Hadley Arkes, professor of political science at Amherst,
and published in the *National Review*, takes issue with the
ACLU's position and argues that a defense of the Nazis'
right to march actually tends to legitimize their organization and views. The crisis precipitated in the ACLU itself
is the subject of the following selection, written by veteran
reporter J. Anthony Lucas and published in the New York
Times Magazine. Professor Arkes' argument is extended
somewhat in the fourth selection, written by William F.
Buckley, Jr., editor of the *National Review* and reprinted
from that publication. In closing, an unsigned article in
the *Nation* essays to give the civil libertarian answer to the
previous commentators.

SKOKIE—THE EXTREME TEST [1]

"Hard cases make bad law" the saying goes. Perhaps.

[1] Article entitled "Right to Be Offensive: Skokie—the Extreme Test," by
Carl Cohen, teacher of philosophy at the University of Michigan, member of the
A.C.L.U., and author of *Democracy* and *Civil Disobedience*. *Nation*. 226::422–8.
Ap. 15 '78. Reprinted by permission of The Nation Associates.

But good principles are rightly tested by extreme cases. The principle that "Congress shall make no law . . . abridging the freedom of speech, or of the press; or the right of the people peaceably to assemble . . ."—than which we have few better—is perennially tested by American Nazis.

The skeletal facts of the latest test are these: The National Socialist Party, under the leadership of Frank Collin, planned public demonstrations in April 1977, in the parks of suburban Chicago. The village of Skokie, four miles north of the Chicago city line, blocked the demonstration within its borders by requiring the prior posting of $350,000 insurance. The Nazis persisted, announcing their intent to march without speeches aimed at any ethnic or racial groups and without distributing literature, but in uniform and with signs and swastikas. Skokie (nearly 60 percent Jewish) then won a court injunction prohibiting the Nazis from displaying their uniforms or swastikas, or disseminating literature, on the date planned. The American Civil Liberties Union, representing the Nazis in this matter, sought but did not get a stay of that injunction from the Illinois Appellate Court. The Illinois Supreme Court refused to hear the case, and the ACLU appealed to the US Supreme Court for a stay of the injunction. That petition was treated by the Supreme Court as one requesting a review of all procedural issues in the case, and granted it, ordering the Illinois courts to respond.

On the narrow question of whether an injunction prohibiting the use of the swastika violated the First Amendment rights of the Nazis the Illinois Supreme Court did respond in January 1978. The injunction was struck down. The Court wrote: "The display of the swastika, as offensive to the principles of a free nation as the memories it recalls may be, is symbolic political speech intended to convey to the public the beliefs of those who display it."

Meanwhile, three new ordinances were adopted by the Skokie Village Council, having much the same effect as the injunction at issue. The first requires a permit for any demonstration of fifty or more persons in the streets or on the sidewalks of Skokie. The second bans "political organizations" from demonstrating in "military style" uniforms. The third bans both the display of "symbols offensive to the community" and the distribution of literature that ascribes a "lack of virtue" to racially or ethnically identifiable groups. Concurrently, a small group of Jews living in Skokie, acting independently of the village and the park district, sought a separate injunction against any Nazi demonstration because of the injury it would allegedly do to them.

That private action the Supreme Court of Illinois ordered dismissed, and the appeal for rehearing has been denied. But the Anti-Defamation League of B'nai B'rith, supporting that private suit, has promised further appeal to the US Supreme Court. The three village ordinances were declared unconstitutional by the Federal District Court in February; but on March 17 that court granted a forty-five-day stay of its own order, as a cooling-off period and to permit the village to appeal the ruling to the 7th Federal Circuit in Chicago. That appeal has been scheduled for late May. The stay (temporarily keeping the ordinances in force) will probably be extended until the 7th Circuit Court reaches a decision on the merits. If that court affirms the District Court (at least on the first two ordinances) the Nazis may march lawfully in late May or June—unless the US Supreme Court grants a further delay.

Citizens on both sides of the controversy are outraged. Is this a hard case? The ACLU does not think so—but by defending the right of the Nazis to demonstrate it has lost some 30 percent of its Illinois membership in a matter of months. The arguments on both sides are more tangled and subtle than is commonly supposed. In the end, however, the ACLU is right: it is not Nazism that is at stake, but the freedom of speech.

Those who would block the Nazi demonstration are not insensitive to the constitutional protection of free speech. They say, in effect:

The freedom of speech—which we honor as fully as does the ACLU—is like every freedom in having limits in a good society.

Defenders of free speech who retain their good sense will realize that Nazis, saying what they say in the way they say it, do exceed reasonable limits. Associating themselves with the literal annihilation of Jews, they now seek to advance their views abrasively in a community populated by many of the very same people who had been tortured by Nazis. Some of these Jews, after narrow escape, have sought refuge in Skokie. We applaud the vigorous defense of controversial speech, but this is a case—given the character of these Nazis and their expressed intent—to which the constitutional protection of dissident opinion does not apply.

This general position of those who would forbid the Nazi demonstration is not sufficient as it stands. Certainly it is true that neither the First Amendment nor any sensible principle lying behind it guarantees the right to say anything, anywhere, at any time. But restrictions upon speech and assembly—especially any that would silence representatives of a political party in a public place with a public aim —must be very narrowly drawn, and face a heavy burden of justification. The task of the Nazi blockers (not "anti-Nazis" because that group surely includes most of those defending the right of Nazis to demonstrate) is to give sound argument specifying the proper limits of free speech that would be exceeded by this demonstration. Every effort to do this while preserving the basic constitutional liberties in question fails, as I shall show.

Grave danger is one limit upon speech thought reasonable by many. Justice Holmes wrote in 1919: "The question in every case is whether the words used are used in such circumstances and are of such a nature as to create a clear and present danger that they will bring about substantive evils that Congress has a right to prevent." [*Schenck* v. *United States*, 249 U.S. 47 at 52.] The village of Skokie applies essentially that standard. It says that the evils of violence resulting from the demonstration are sure, the danger of them patently clear, and (were the Nazis to march) immediately present. Holmes's justly famous illustration makes the point vividly: "The most stringent protection of free speech would not protect a man in falsely shouting fire in a theatre, and causing a panic:" Nazis waving swastikas in a mainly Jewish community, say the people of Skokie, are in effect shouting fire in a theater. That irresponsible use of speech we are not obliged to permit; neither the shouter in the theater nor the Nazi in the street is entitled to the constitutional protection of free speech.

The analogy is seriously flawed. Whoever falsely shouts fire in a theater is certainly not entitled to free-speech protection. But the circumstances of a Nazi demonstration differ from those of the theater in three fundamental respects.

First, the theater audience is captive, subjected against its will to the shout and its sequel. Not so any gathering for a Nazi parade or demonstration. Those angered or offended are free to stay away, or to leave; they need have nothing to do with the affair. The panic in the theater traps and injures those present for reasons entirely unrelated to the shout: that false alarm is not essentially speech at all; it is no different from the fraudulent ringing of an alarm bell. Of the audience any Nazi march may draw, all this simply cannot be said.

Second, the shouted warning is of such a nature that it permits no discussion. It is not the expression of an opinion but a signal for flight, giving no opportunity for reasoned reply. The Nazi demonstration may be answered with counter-demonstrations; it may be refuted, in print or by voice; then or later. Nazi demonstrators offer no threat of immediate calamity comparable to that of a false alarm in a crowded hall.

Third, the alarm in the theater is, by hypothesis, false; we would think very differently of an honest warning. Nazi views are also false, no doubt, but being right is not a condition on which permission to demonstrate may be premised. Who should have that permission if it were? And who decide?

Some words, in some special circumstances, because of the grave danger they immediately create, cannot claim the protection of free speech. Shouting fire falsely in a theater is one such case; a political demonstration in a park, by Nazis or anyone else is not.

"But," rejoins the Nazi blocker, "you underestimate the seriousness of the threat this demonstration immediately creates. If the Nazis march in Skokie with swastikas and brown shirts they will almost certainly provoke a riot. Incitement to riot is a crime. When it is deliberate, as in this case, when its violent consequences are highly probable and fully anticipated, such incitement cannot be defended as mere speech. It is conduct designed to breach the public peace, using the First Amendment as shield. Skokie has the right, even the duty, to protect itself against the threat of that despicable design."

This dangerous argument seriously misapprehends the concept of incitement to riot. The fact that a message or symbol excites an audience to furious antagonism gives no evidence whatever of criminal incitement. That crime consists in urging upon one's audience the commission of some unlawful act in a context in which it is probable that some in the audience will do what is being urged. Even then the speaker will not normally be guilty of criminal incitement unless persons in his audience do in fact engage in the unlawful conduct he urged upon them. Nothing like those conditions is present in this case. Nazi speakers shrewdly plan to urge nothing explicitly unlawful. ("Free speech for the white man" was their announced slogan for this occasion.) They urge no specific acts at all, certainly no illegal ones. In a fury directed at the Nazis, some in the Skokie audience may subsequently break the law—but those whose symbols provoked their fury cannot be legally responsible for the misconduct. In the interests of freedom, incitement must be very narrowly delineated. When overt unlawful deeds are committed as a direct consequence of agitating speech, that speech becomes part of the crime—as the planning of an actual robbery becomes part of that robbery. Persons whose inflammatory words lead immediately to the disorder they propose may be similarly culpable. But the

Nazis, few of whose audience will be inclined to do anything they may urge, could never be guilty, in Skokie, of inciting to riot.

"Regarding the technical conditions for that crime you may be correct," the Nazi blocker continues,

but you are blinded by technicalities. The Nazis delight in creating fright and havoc among Jews. Recently in this country their demonstrations have several times actually resulted in riot. Nazis understand full well how maddening their symbols are to their intended victims; they plan that abrasion. It is a good principle in law that one may reasonably be held to intend the natural and expected consequences of one's acts. True, the riot will not be caused by an audience that complies with the urgings of Nazi agitators. The Nazis may thus be innocent of some narrowly defined crime of "incitement." They will nevertheless be guilty of engaging deliberately in conduct designed to infuriate and calculated to result in a wholesale breach of the public peace. From incitement in that more general sense we can and must protect ourselves.

This argument, having much prima facie appeal, is the one on which Skokie chiefly relies. But the village is profoundly mistaken when it assumes that speakers may be silenced because of the response expected to their words. If that were granted, no truly controversial position on an incendiary topic could be freely presented. When it could be shown that the probable reaction would be intemperate or disorderly, the advocacy of an unpopular position would have to be forbidden. Thus, tying the permissibility of controversial speech to its expected reception by an audience establishes what has been called "the heckler's veto." A society that honors freedom concretely cannot authorize that veto.

Very unpopular causes may be as freely advocated under our Constitution as those in popular favor. Aberrant political advocates, progressive or reactionary, wise or crazy, will commonly meet with an angry and unruly reception. Communists, pacifists, National Socialists—especially those on the extreme of any continuum—will be forever in need of defense. Their freedom is our interest not only because our side may one day meet similar response but because rational judgment upon any position requires that it be heard. Some lessons must be repeatedly relearned, even by those who once taught them. If the Nazis are not free to speak because their Jewish audience will be hostile, the Jews will not be free to speak when their Arab audience promises equal hostility. When demonstrations to which sufficient ire may be threatened are not allowed, the hecklers have a veto—and they have it whatever the content of their views.

The issue has been tested. A passionate message of racial hatred was delivered—also in Chicago, in 1949, by a Catholic priest under suspension—to a sizable audience in a large hall. Outside, a cordon of police struggled to control the infuriated counter-demonstrators, while Father Terminiello completed his speech. He was later convicted for creating a breach of the peace—a breach created not by him or his followers but by persons outside the lecture hall so maddened by his bigotry as to throw bottles and bricks at the windows as he spoke. Is Father Terminiello to be legally punished for speaking so? The judge in the trial court had instructed the jury that the words "breach of the peace" include speech that "stirs the public to anger, invites dispute, brings about a condition of unrest, or creates a disturbance. . . ." That, said the Supreme Court, was grave error. Justice Douglas wrote the majority opinion:

[One] function of free speech under our system of government is to invite dispute. It may indeed best serve its high purpose when it induces a condition of unrest, creates dissatisfaction with conditions as they are, or even stirs people to anger. Speech is often provocative and challenging. It may strike at prejudices and preconceptions and have profound unsettling effects as it presses for acceptance of an idea. That is why freedom of speech, though not absolute, . . . is nevertheless protected against censorship or punishment, unless shown likely to produce a clear and present danger of a serious substantive evil that rises far above public inconvenience, annoyance, or unrest. [*Terminiello* v. *City of Chicago*, 337 U.S. 1, at 4, 149.]

The right of a racist to speak freely becomes a bulwark for all. Civil rights activists, convicted a few years later because of the tumultuous responses of their hostile audiences, had their convictions also reversed by the Supreme Court, relying on the *Terminiello* decision. Even in the most hostile territory the right to political agitation for all parties has been secured.

The case for the Nazis is stronger than that for Terminiello, whose angry opponents really did throw bricks. Nothing has been thrown at the Nazis in Skokie because they have not yet been allowed to speak there. The mere threat of disorder has served to silence political speech. An injunction based on that threat encourages continuing threats and further restrictions. Such prior restraint of speech is highly objectionable. It does not allow even for the test of the impact of that speech. In the *Pentagon Papers* case, the claim by the United States Government that publication of the papers would lead to loss of life in Southeast Asia was rightly rejected by the Supreme Court as ground for an injunction prohibiting publication in advance. Should that Court tolerate an injunction forbidding in advance a controversial demonstration on domestic public affairs?

"They should even if they won't," replies the Nazi blocker, "when that speech has a very high probability of provoking violence. We cannot know with absolute certainty what the future holds; we cannot be absolutely sure that a riot will ensue if the Nazis parade with swastikas in Skokie. But we can be confident when we predict it. Some words and symbols, by their plain meaning in known contexts, are so provocative as to cause decent and reasonable people to respond by fighting. Speech like that is rightly forbidden.

"In this, the Supreme Court is on our side. A Jehovah's Witness named Chaplinsky, convicted in New Hampshire for shouting at a policeman, when stopped from preaching in the street: 'You are a goddamned racketeer [and] a damned Fascist and the whole government of Rochester are Fascists or agents of Fascists,' claimed freedom of speech as his shield

unsuccessfully. Some utterances, the Supreme Court said, are not entitled to normal protection.

[I]t is well understood that the right of free speech is not absolute at all times and under all circumstances. There are certain well-defined and narrowly limited classes of speech, the prevention and punishment of which have never been thought to raise any constitutional problem. These include the lewd and obscene, the profane, the libelous, and the insulting or "fighting words"—those which by their very utterance inflict injury or tend to incite an immediate breach of the peace. [*Chaplinsky* v. *New Hampshire*, 315 U.S. 568, at 572, 1942.]

"That fighting words should not be protected as normal verbal controversy," the blocker concludes, "is plain good sense. In a community where live thousands of survivors of Nazi death camps, an aggressive Nazi demonstration is surely speech which, by its very utterance, inflicts injury and tends to incite an immediate breach of the peace."

The argument fails utterly. The doctrine applied—that words themselves are sometimes to be treated as equivalent to the first physical blows in a fight—is highly suspect. What words under what circumstances may be treated so must be forever disputable. Words can hurt, but there is a difference between a verbal and a physical blow that metaphor must not be allowed to blur. If the words that sometimes provoke a fight are silenced, the general uncertainty about which words may have that effect must chill all debate, hedge all robust speaking in vigorous contest. The theory that nasty words justify immediate physical retaliation is a bad one— and, in fact, it is a theory now almost universally abandoned.

Even if accepted in the extreme case, however, the application of the "fighting-words" doctrine would have to be so narrowly restricted to special circumstances as to have no bearing on a proposed demonstration by Nazis. It could apply only to utterances by one person to the face of another, being defamatory in the extreme. Political demonstrations before a general public, however despicable the views presented, are not one-to-one situations. Moreover the doctrine could apply (if ever) only after those insults were hurled and a retaliatory blow struck—clearly not the present case. Above all, the "fighting-words" doctrine, if applicable in any context, would be so only as a consequence of some personal offense, never when the cause of agitation, however bitter, is political. The gambit cannot succeed.

"Yet we all know," the Nazi blocker rejoins, "that Nazi propaganda will be exceedingly painful in this context. The expression 'fighting words' may be inexact here, but it points to the heart of the case, the real ground upon which an injunction prohibiting a Nazi demonstration in Skokie is justifiable. The Nazis may or may not begin a fight, or incite disorder, or breach the public peace—but it is certainly the case that, if they march and speak, they will do severe and irreparable harm to a substantial number of Jews—refugees from the Third Reich—now living in Skokie.

"It is not the speech as such that we ask to have enjoined, but the deliberate injury of those living their post-Holocaust lives in mutual company and refuge. By demonstrating in storm-trooper style the Nazis will inflict—and seek to inflict—direct personal pain upon those who have once already been their innocent victims. The infliction of such injury no community is obliged to permit."

Of all objections to the Nazi demonstrations this is the most serious. It is advanced not by the village of Skokie but by a small group of Jewish survivors living there, and it relies, sensitively, upon what appears to distinguish this case from all ordinary cases of controversial speech. Consider this argument in greater detail:

(a) "The atrocities to which the victims of the Holocaust were subjected cannot be captured in words. For the present it may be enough to say that the mother of one of the plaintiffs in this case was murdered by the Nazis, having been thrown into a well with fifty other women while alive, and covered with gravel. To the perpetrators of this and a thousand like crimes the American Nazis give proud allegiance."

(b) "Upon the few surviving victims the Nazis inflicted a psychological trauma so profound as to scar their lives forever. Overwhelming anxiety, recurrent terror, paralyzing helplessness, emotional anguish—all manifested not only in mental suffering but in physical pain and disorder—flow still from those cruelties. Nazi anti-Semitism cannot pass as ordinary political controversy."

(c) "The Nazis' specific intent to pursue the Jews taking refuge in America—to arouse and marshal hatred of them—was plainly announced in a leaflet they distributed just prior to the planned march:

. . . we have decided to relocate in areas heavily populated by the real enemy—the Jews!
An old maxim goes: "Where one finds the most Jews, there also shall one find the most Jew-haters." With this basic truth in mind, we are now planning a number of street demonstrations and even speeches in Evanston, Skokie, Lincolnwood, North Shore, Morton Grove, etc. . . . Our successful opposition to the Black Invasion of Southwest Chicago will now be turned on the culprits who started it all: The Jews!"

(d) "The survivors, if subjected now to demonstrations earlier witnessed by them personally in connection with their earlier torture, will be caused great emotional harm no matter what they do—whether they counter-demonstrate, stay in their homes, or attempt to go about their business as if nothing painful were taking place. There is remedy at law for such deliberate injury. The Illinois Supreme Court (among others) has made it clear that the intentional infliction of severe emotional distress does give a right to redress. Two conditions must be met:

(1) 'The aggressive invasion of mental equanimity' must be 'unwarranted and unprovoked,' and (2) it must be calculated to cause severe emotional disturbance in the person of ordinary sensibilities, or there must be 'special knowledge or notice' of atypical sensibilities. [*Knierim* v. *Izzo*, 174 N.E. 2d, 157, at 165, 1961.]

"That Nazis have special knowledge of the atypical vulnerability of the Jewish survivors in Skokie is beyond question. Indeed, they planned the demonstration precisely there because that is where the Jews are. Nor is there any doubt that the first condition is also met. What provocation by the Jews warrants the Nazis' carefully planned attack upon them? What could be a clearer instance of the aggressive invasion of mental equanimity of innocent citizens? As a legal matter, as well as a moral one, the conditions of redress are surely present."

(e) "But may a court anticipate the need for redress by enjoining the demonstration before it takes place? Yes, it may when what the demonstrators plan to do can be shown to cause irreparable damage if allowed. 'A state has the right to curtail free speech,' an Illinois Appellate Court has written, 'when . . . it determines that such curtailment is necessary to protect the public interest. . . .' [*Jersey County Motor Co.* v. *Teamsters Local 525*, 156 N.E. 2d, 633, at 636, 1959.] The public interest at stake is evident. These survivors of Nazi terror, most of them elderly, sought sanctuary in Skokie. The invasion of that refuge would result in injury to them for which no remedy could then be purchased at any price. Citizens (to use the words of earlier court decisions) cannot expect protection from 'mere vulgarities' or 'meaningless abusive expressions' or 'trivialities and mere bad manners.' And in weighing the impact of the speech a distinction must be drawn between symptoms of emotional distress 'visible to the professional eye' and 'neurotic overreactions to trivial hurts.' Granted. Who doubts which side of that line the consequences of a Nazi demonstration in Skokie would fall?"

(f) "It will be said that there is no precedent for such curtailment of speech by court injunction. But no earlier set of facts is anything like these. There is no precedent for the horror of the Nazi campaign against the Jews, and there is no precedent for their publicly announced intention to prey upon their victims by calling vividly to mind the cruelties earlier done to them. 'No person,' the Illinois Supreme Court has said, 'has a right to make war on another.' [*Carpenters' Union* v. *Citizens' Committee*, 164 N.E. 393, at 401, 1928.] The Nazis make war on the Jews. They have done so, brutally, for decades; now, in Skokie, they announce their intention to do so again. There never was anything like this."

The persuasiveness of this argument depends upon its transition from the pain the Nazi demonstration may cause to the action proposed to prevent it. At issue here is not historical fact but the claim that the potential hurt of recalling it justifies the prohibition of a political demonstration. It does not. Three points:

First. Freedoms simply do not come without cost. For the freedom of speech the cost is often substantial, and sometimes its burden must be unevenly borne. Where speech is genuinely free there must be a collective commitment to accept the consequences of that freedom. Painful and offensive utterances, some cruelly unfair, will be openly aired. Reputations will suffer, sometimes unjustly; old wounds will be opened, sometimes viciously. Our choice is between the protection of freedom with the acceptance of its costs, on the one hand, and the protection of personal sensitivities (and the alleged sensitivities of those in power) at the price of sharply restricting the public forum, on the other hand. That choice has essentially been made by the American body politic. The Nazi blocker would make another.

How great the pain will be for the Jews in Skokie is hard to say. That the public appearance of some fanatic young Nazis would reactivate all the terrors of thirty years before may be an exaggeration. Great anger will be refreshed; that may not be unhealthy. Vigorous counter-demonstrations and the expressed contempt for the Nazis by an articulate press may prove a satisfying balm. Neither pluses nor minuses can be quantified. If there is a nonmeasurable balance on the negative side—which is uncertain—that is one of the unavoidable costs of an open society.

Victims of Stalinism cannot avoid its repeated advocacy. Victims of racism may not silence a racist who teaches their genetic inferiority. Those believing organized religion to be cruel superstition have no more authority to suppress it than have religionists the authority to suppress satanic apostasy. The field of open argument—serious, angry, important argument—runs with blood from psychic wounds.

Second. Of all such costs none is so clearly entailed by the democratic process as that arising from open advocacy of a political party, however crazy or extreme. Hate them as we may, the denial that the Nazis are a party will not stand examination. On the fringe of madness they may be, but that has been said, and will be said, of every revolutionary view. We simply cannot silence a party—any party—and expect to remain free.

Third. Psychic pain, even if so great and deliberate as to be cause for redress cannot ground the prior restraint of speech. Much of what is feared from the exercise of freedom never transpires. The constitution of an open society—not its document merely but the basic principles of its life—precludes the silencing of some out of concern for the sensibilities of others. This is not callousness but a condition of the democratic process.

Finally, the Nazi blocker must face the fact that it is not harm to some, or danger to all, or incitement to riot, or fighting words, or any such concern that chiefly motivates him. It is the evil of these Nazi views, their blatant racism and anti-Semitism, that he thinks deserves to be silenced. When other arguments have failed he comes in the end to question the principle of free speech itself, asking, in effect, whether that principle really does oblige us to protect all content, however damnable. This is his last resort:

Some speech content—speech utterly without redeeming social value—is not and ought not be protected by the First Amendment. Hard-core obscenity, as one example, does not come under its umbrella. Obscenity, of course, is normally associated with sexually explicit matter. But its essential, nonsexual characteristics are two: it is intolerably offensive in some settings, and it is totally worthless. Whatever may go on behind closed doors, not every form of language, or picture, or act is permitted in public places. Lewd depictions of perverted behavior, actual sexual intercourse, or other such matter is forbidden in public. Its prohibition is based on the recognition that thrusting that specific content upon an unwilling audience in a public place is a gross imposition and a cause of offense against which they (and all of us) have a right to be protected. Such matter does not contribute in any way to the political forum. It is barren of ideas, 'not in any proper sense communication of information or opinion safeguarded by the Constitution' as the Supreme Court wrote of some forms of expression not to be protected. [*Chaplinsky* v. *New Hampshire*, 315 U.S. 568, at 572, 1942.]

Nazi garbage, although not in the same way carnal, is just like that. Citizens of a decent community have the right to be shielded against it in precisely that spirit. Indeed, the intrinsic offensiveness of lascivious acts or pictures is minor compared to that of the public thrusting of irrational racism and anti-Semitism. Its worthlessness is manifest. We contend, therefore, that in a wide but accurate sense of the term, Nazi hate-mongering is obscene. As that category is used in law, we realize, it would not here apply. But it is no stretch of language or concept to call it that, and it is no unreasonable stretch of law to prohibit its presentation on the same fundamental grounds.

All censorship comes to this in the end: some content is so very bad that it must not be heard or seen. The root of the issue between blocker and libertarian is here exposed. We may prevent the Nazi demonstration, the blocker believes in his heart, because those views are utterly intolerable. If anything is nearly intolerable, the libertarian believes in his heart, it is that argument from badness—giving the power to silence to those who do not like what they hear. The Nazis provide a splendid illustration. Called manifestly worthless, their views in fact are laden with ideas, many of them despicable, but for that very reason highly meaningful. No segment of the community is entitled to decide for the rest of us that any ideas are so lacking in merit as to be excluded from the public forum.

Even where the matter in question has no political content, and is sexually explicit, and is known to give offense to some in the community, we protect the freedom of others to see and hear by obliging those who are offended to shield themselves by turning away, or walking away. Precisely this issue was faced by the Supreme Court in 1975, when it held

invalid a city ordinance that prohibited films "in which
the human male or female bare buttocks, human female
bare breasts, or human bare pubic areas are shown, if such
motion picture, slide, or other exhibits is visible from any
public street or place." [*Erznoznik* v. *City of Jacksonville*,
422 U.S. 205, at 207, 1975.] When it is possible for a viewer
or hearer to turn away, the Court concluded, his being offended when he does not do so will not serve to cancel the
rights of speakers. Justice Powell:

> A State or municipality may protect individual privacy by en-
> acting reasonable time, place, and manner regulations applicable
> to all speech irrespective of content. . . . But when the govern-
> ment, acting as censor, undertakes selectively to shield the public
> from some kinds of speech on the ground that they are more
> offensive than others, the First Amendment strictly limits its
> power. . . . Such selective restrictions have been upheld only when
> the speaker intrudes on the privacy of the home . . . or the degree
> of captivity makes it impractical for the unwilling viewer or au-
> ditor to avoid exposure. [p. 209.]

An earlier case—in which a young man was vindicated
in his right to wear, in a courthouse, a jacket emblazoned
with the words "Fuck the Draft"—is cited in support: "The
ability of government, consonant with the Constitution, to
shut off discourse solely to prevent others from hearing it is
. . . dependent upon a showing that substantial privacy interests are being invaded in an essentially intolerable manner. Any broader view of this authority would effectively
empower a majority to silence dissidents simply as a matter
of personal predilections." [*Cohen* v. *California*, 403 U.S.
15, at 21, 1971.]

Would the privacy rights of Skokie residents be invaded
by a Nazi demonstration in an essentially intolerable manner? Surely not. Persons in their homes are entitled to protection from the intrusive noise of sound trucks blasting so
as to reach them no matter what they do. But parks and
streets are the common and proper place for political assembly. To some degree we cannot avoid encountering what

happens in such places, but we do not have to stay; and we cannot expect to be insulated by law from all that we find intensively objectionable. Justice Powell continues:

The plain, if at times disquieting, truth is that in our pluralistic society, constantly proliferating new and ingenious forms of expression, "we are inescapably captive audiences for many purposes." . . . Much that we encounter offends our aesthetic, if not our political and moral, sensibilities. Nevertheless, the Constitution does not permit government to decide which types of otherwise protected speech are sufficiently offensive to require protection for the unwilling listener or viewer. Rather, absent the narrow circumstances described above [in which exposure is impossible to avoid] the burden normally falls upon the viewer to "avoid further bombardment of [his] sensibilities simply by averting [his] eyes." [422 U.S. 210.] The screen of a drive-in theatre is not so obtrusive as to make it impossible for an unwilling individual to avoid exposure to it. The "limited privacy interests of persons on the public streets cannot justify . . . censorship of otherwise protected speech on the basis of its content."

"Well," comes the last rejoinder from the blocker, "*is* this otherwise protected speech? By calling attention to its offensiveness and worthlessness we have shown that it, like hardcore obscenity, is not entitled to protection. Hence the legitimacy of restricting it."

But the right of the public to see the Nazis and hear what they say is at least as compelling as the right to look at bare buttocks and breasts. Nudity and sex, some hold, when enjoyed in print and pictures for themselves alone, are utterly without redeeming social value and for that reason not entitled to free-speech protection. That argument, very questionable respecting even hard-core pornography, is patently inapplicable to political matter.

Political debate—"uninhibited, robust, and wide open," in parks and streets as well as lecture halls—will rouse anger and give offense. Public offensiveness, like private distress, is an unavoidable cost of freedom. Citizens who would govern themselves have the right to hear every opinion on their public business. That the Nazis may be vicious or crazy does not cancel our need to pass judgment upon their views. Their speech is protected, as all political speech is protected, partly as a matter of their right, partly as a matter of course.

Exceptions cannot be made for nasty opinions. If the swastika is too offensive for some to tolerate today, the Star of David will be claimed equally intolerable by others tomorrow. These marchers have the same right to sing the "Horst Wessel Lied" as others have to sing the "Internationale" or "We Shall Overcome." The answer to the argument from badness is not that the symbols complained of are not offensive but that offense of that sort cannot justify prohibiting their display in public places.

The effectiveness of public protest often depends critically upon the symbolic use of location. The Nazis would march in Skokie just because it is heavily Jewish. Think of them what we may, that is part of their political point. Civil rights demonstrators, as part of their point, often carried their moral convictions—very offensive to the segregationist majority—to the heart of Jim Crow country, to Selma, Alabama, and Philadelphia, Mississippi. Blacks who demonstrate for fair-housing opportunity bring their protests to the heart of the suburban communities that would exclude them. If we will not protect Nazis carrying "White Power" signs in black neighborhoods, how shall we protect Black Panthers carrying "Black Power" signs in white neighborhoods?

But civil rights marchers carried the banner of decency, while the swastika is the symbol of unspeakable indecency. Yes. That judgment, however, has no bearing on the right to speak publicly. If the history of struggles to defend the freedom of thought and expression teaches anything it teaches this: that persons or parties must not be silenced because of the moral qualities their views are judged to have. Our best hope that public judgment passed upon the Nazis will prove sound rests upon the freedom of all to hear them and all to speak in reply. By presenting the extreme case these Nazis provide an instructive test of a very good principle.

MARCHING THROUGH SKOKIE [2]

Will the Nazis finally march in Skokie? They have sought to stage their demonstration in the suburbs of Chicago since May of last year [1977], and until very recently there seemed to be a concert between the state and Federal courts to strike down every legal obstacle that might have prevented the Nazis from marching. But suddenly the declamations were suspended and judicial minds were concentrated anew, with the mounting evidence that other groups would be coming to Skokie with the intention of meeting the Nazis in the street with a show of violence. In February, Judge Bernard Decker of the Federal District Court had swept away the restrictions on the Nazis and warned against the danger of "permitting the government to decide what its citizens may say and hear." By the end of March, however, Judge Decker issued a restraining order to postpone the demonstration (and, presumably, the "principle" he articulated) for another 45 days.

In this manner the courts have managed to create the worst of all possible worlds. They have been given the chance over several months to restrain the Nazis on grounds of jurisprudential principles that are fundamental to a democratic order. What they chose to do instead was to affirm the view that a democracy has *no* principles by which to judge the Nazis—but then to restrain the Nazis anyway without the benefit of principles: the courts have established now that the Nazis have the wildest claims to constitutional freedom, but that their freedom of expression may be restricted so long as hostile groups show a willingness to use violence. The result, in short, has been decidedly anti-libertarian. Instead of using the occasion to teach something about the principles that define legitimate interests and expression, the courts have given credence to the most

[2] Article by Hadley Arkes, professor of political science at Amherst and author of *The Moral Foundations of Urban Politics*. National Review. 30:588–93. My. 12, '78. Reprinted by permission of *National Review*, 150 E. 35th St. New York, NY 10016.

cynical understanding of the law—viz., that the law is merely a polite form in which the force of the many may govern the few.

But of course it is not the mission of the Nazis to attach the people ever more strongly to the institutions and laws of a democratic society, and so whether they march or not, they will have accomplished a large portion of their ends: they will have caused urbane citizens of all classes to regard the courts as witless and the laws as amoral.

The choice of Skokie as a target was clearly not inadvertent. Of the 69,000 people in Skokie, about 40,000 are Jews, and of the Jewish refugees from Europe who came to Chicago between 1930 and 1960, most are thought to have settled in Skokie. A group called Survivors of the Holocaust was organized in the metropolitan area, and of the 12,000 members of this group, 7,000 were living in Skokie. Skokie was not chosen by the Nazis, then, because it was the most promising place in which to recruit new members or hold a discussion about the substantive "program" of the party. The aim of the march, very plainly, was to gather attention and create an effect that was well out of proportion to the actual size of the group (which apparently comprises thirty to fifty members). The Nazis could easily accomplish that end by marching into a community of Jews with the full trappings of their symbolism —the uniforms, the caps, the swastikas on arms and flags; by presenting, in short, the kind of spectacle that should elicit outrage among decent people of any persuasion, and by counting on the fact that the public outrage would be sure to attract the attention of the media.

As recently as 15 years ago in this country, this kind of spectacle would have been seen perfectly clearly for what it was: a deliberate attempt to provoke a population to violence—which is to say, an attempt to provoke *without justification*. It was well understood that the entrance of the police or clergy into a tough neighborhood could provoke the local denizens to fury, but that was not the kind of provocation from which the law sought to protect people. What the law sought to proscribe were demonstrations that stood, in effect, as assaults, and it was hard to find a professor of law who was not alert to these differences. Even the most committed civil libertarians were willing to concede that the law might properly restrain the Ku Klux Klan if that organization sought to stage an entertainment for its own benefit by marching through Harlem. And what was plausible to most of our own scholars of law barely more than a decade ago has remained plausible to the friends of constitutional government in other countries. The British were compelled to make use of their authority in Northern Ireland a few years ago to stop a series of reciprocal provocative marches by Protestants into Catholic areas and Catholics into Protestant areas—marches that persistently sparked violence, and that were conceived with that purpose in mind.

It was in this tradition of governing demonstrations in the streets that the village of Skokie sought an injunction to restrain the Nazis, and the injunction was granted by a county court. The injunction was later amended slightly to prohibit the Nazis from marching or parading with their uniforms and insignia, and (according to one report) "from distributing pamphlets or displaying any materials that incite or promote hatred against persons of Jewish faith or ancestry or other persons." After a series of appeals to the highest courts at the state and federal levels, these restrictions were struck down and the injunction dissolved. In the meantime, though, another injunction was sought against the Nazis by residents of Skokie who were survivors of the Holocaust. These people claimed that the advent of the Nazis to their neighborhood would be the source of a special injury or emotional strain for them by reviving many of the traumas they associated with their experience in the war. This suit is still making its way through the courts.

Ordinarily one can hope that the expense and fatigue of litigation may generate their own benign effects; but the Nazis have been buoyed up in this long process by the support—and the special skills—of the American Civil Liberties Union. The implications of this support have not been lost on Jewish members of the ACLU, and the reaction has been so severe that the ACLU has lost (by some accounts) nearly 25 per cent of its members. All of this, however, may simply confirm to the leaders of the ACLU that the sensibilities they possess on these matters are not commonly distributed among the population at large, or even among most of their own sustaining members.

For the leadership of the ACLU, it would be accurate to say that there is ultimately no "truth" in matters political —that all ideas about the proper form of government over men come to rest at the end on personal beliefs or opinions, which cannot finally be measured as true or false. As far at least as the right to speak is concerned, the case for a regime of law and the case for a regime of genocide must be counted, in this view, as equally deserving of a claim *to be heard* and (ultimately) approved by the public. David Hamlin, the executive director of the Illinois division of the ACLU, was moved to say, regarding the Nazis, that "the First Amendment . . . affords us the unique opportunity to hear every *imaginable* idea, and to voice our opinions on any one. *It protects all ideas—popular or despised,* good or bad . . . so that each of us can make a free and intelligent choice." (Emphasis added.) In Mr. Hamlin's understanding, it is a matter of being "popular" *or* "despised": to be despised is to be "unpopular." It is apparently no part of his own understanding that certain things are in themselves, in principle, despicable.

Mr. Hamlin is quite plain on the point that we must be free to hear the Nazis in order to preserve our freedom to *choose* the Nazis if we wish. But of course the Constitution was never meant to be neutral in this way about the choice between despotism and free government. The Founders understood that the case for government by consent began with a self-evident truth grounded in nature; as Madison put it during the first Congress, the natural equality of human beings—their capacity for self-governing—had to be understood as an "absolute truth." And if the political order was indeed established on a necessary, self-evident truth, the perspective represented by the Nazis simply cannot be treated for a moment as plausible and legitimate. It cannot be regarded as plausible, that is, without calling into question the truth of those premises on which all constitutional rights depend. In the last analysis, then, it is a mistake to pretend that the Constitution is indifferent to the character and ends of the Nazis.

What the Constitution commends, however, may be one thing; what the Supreme Court has wrought in recent years is another. At this moment our law faces in two directions. On the one hand the Supreme Court has eroded those standards that the law has used over the years to restrain assaults carried out through speech or expression. A majority of the Court has even gone so far as to suggest that there is no principled way to mark off forms of speech that are insulting or defamatory, as against forms of speech that are neutral or inoffensive. Working on this assumption, the Court has made it very difficult to sustain any local ordinance on "provocative" and insulting speech, and, as a result of the decisions that have been taken in this vein over the last seven years, it does in fact become harder to restrain the Nazis in their march in Skokie.

But on the other hand the Court has never overturned the precedents that provided the foundation at an earlier time for the restriction of injurious speech. In fact, the Court has found it necessary in recent years to firm up its commitments to those older precedents; when it comes to the matter of confirming the power of local governments to restrain obscenity and public lewdness, the Court has been compelled to explain, in a more traditional, familiar voice, that not all forms of speech and expression can claim the protection of the Constitution.

The authority that the Court cites most importantly on these occasions is the classic case of *Chaplinsky* v. *New*

Hampshire, which was decided by a unanimous Court in 1942. In the passage that is cited most often from that case, Justice Murphy argued for the Court that

there are certain well-defined and narrowly limited classes of speech, the prevention and punishment of which have never been thought to raise any constitutional problem. These include the lewd and obscene, the profane, the libelous, and the insulting or "fighting" words—those which *by their utterance inflict injury* or tend to incite an immediate breach of the peace. It has been well observed that such utterances are *no essential part of any exposition of ideas,* and are of such slight social value as a step to truth that any benefit that may be derived from them is clearly outweighed by the social interest in order and morality. [Emphasis added.]

When the ACLU came to offer its brief for the Nazis in Skokie it insisted that the concept of "fighting" words applied only to personal epithets that arose in "face-to-face" encounters. For some reason it seemed to be assumed that these personal encounters were more likely to "incite an immediate breach of the peace" (more likely, say, than attacks that were made on a whole racial or religious group). At the same time, since the test in *Chaplinsky* was narrowed to assaults of the most personal nature, it was argued that the holding was not meant to cover speech with a larger political significance. In these interpretations the ACLU was essentially following the direction of the Court in recent years, as a majority of the Court has sought to narrow the holding in *Chaplinsky.* But as the four Nixon appointees have continued to point out in dissent, that novel rendering leaves out half of the formula in *Chaplinsky*—and the part that has given *Chaplinsky* its fuller reach and significance.

Justice Murphy had not limited the holding in *Chaplinsky* to speech of a merely personal nature that was likely to elicit violence. His judgment also encompassed words "which by their utterance inflict injury," even if they are not accompanied by overt acts that involve a physical assault. In that respect the opinion served to remind us that, in the strictest understanding of the law, "assaults" have not required bodily contact; they may be carried out just as effectively by assailants who deliberately stop short of touching the victim's body, as in the case of one who strikes at a person and intentionally misses, or one who points a loaded—or for that matter even an unloaded—pistol at another person. The assaults in these acts are implicit in the gestures, and they may be punished even without waiting for bodily injury.

In that sense the case helped to remind us, too, that there is such a thing as psychological injury or shock, which may be quite as grave—and as much of a concern in the eyes of the law—as an assault on one's body, or a broken leg. When all of these points were taken together, the *Chaplinsky* case suggested in a rather compelling way that people had a claim to be protected from unprovoked or unjustified assaults (including verbal or psychological assaults) when they ventured into a public place.

That is not all there was, of course, to the *Chaplinsky* case, but it does suggest the features that have made *Chaplinsky* a case of such enduring importance. In a far more satisfying manner than any other court decision, *Chaplinsky* was able to account for the grounds on which we would be justified in calling the police, for example, and ordering a crowd to "move along" in those cases where nearly everyone would agree that the crowd *should,* in decency, be dispersed, even though there is only speech or expression involved. One need only imagine, in a hypothetical case, that a crowd gathers before the house of the first black family to move into the neighborhood. No violence is initiated; no rocks or bottles are thrown. The crowd merely stands there, perhaps chanting in a low tone, and, as the day wears on, the crowd may go long stretches in which it makes no sound at all. There is no breach of the peace, nor even anything that fits the usual notion of a public disturbance. But when the people leave the house they have to face the crowd, and the crowd simply stands there, intimidating by its very presence.

Since the crowd refrains from violence it might be said
that it is engaged in a "peaceable assembly" or perhaps even
a form of public protest. For despite the fact that the
harassment is aimed at a private family, the gathering of
the crowd has a larger political significance: the aim of the
crowd, quite clearly, is to have an effect on the character
of the community by keeping blacks out. In pursuing this
form of intimidation outside the law, the object is to dis-
courage the members of the family from exercising rights
that are theirs in the law, and perhaps also to frustrate the
ends of a public policy that seeks to bring down the bar-
riers to racial integration. The fact that the crowd refrains
from speech or discussion is not enough in itself to reduce
the event to an instance of "conduct" rather than "speech":
it has already been established over a long train of cases
that "expression" may cover symbolic acts or gestures that
involve no speech or writing at all: e.g., the rendering of a
flag salute, the burning of a draft card, the wearing of an
armband.

If the police intervened and dispersed the crowd outside
the house, they would clearly be restricting political expression; and yet it should be apparent that the police would
be quite justified in intervening. But if the law can reach
a case of this kind it is because it is possible to recognize
the nature of the words and gestures themselves, *in the
context in which they are used,* and understand that they
were meant to intimidate or assault.

There has never been any serious doubt that speech
bears a special significance in a republican system. Republican government begins with the understanding that
the exercise of political power over others must be justified, and it sets about to ensure, through a variety of devices, that people in positions of authority are compelled
to offer justifications for themselves. The politics of a republic is a politics that takes place through a public discourse over political things. As our own Founders understood, it is very important, then, for a republic to preserve
a proper freedom of discussion about the central concerns

of politics—i.e., about the conditions of justice in the society and the substantive ends of the state. The freedom to engage in discussion would be as large as any other freedom properly exercised. It would be restrained only in those instances in which it became the vehicle of injury (or "injustice") to others. At that moment, however, speech could claim no more protection than any other mode of freedom. The Founders rejected the rule of the censor and the convention of "prior restraint" on publication. But they were uniform in their denunciation of a "licentious" press, and they assumed that the laws on defamation (both civil and criminal) would function as a form of redress against the injuries that were inflicted through speech.

And so, while the Founders understood that a republican regime was a regime of public discourse and conflict, they understood also that a republican regime was a regime of law before it was anything else. As a regime of law its first obligation was to render justice: to protect its citizens against harms that were inflicted on them unjustly, outside a process of law.

When it comes, therefore, to the American Nazis and their freedom of expression, the obligations of the regime are nowhere near as one-sided as libertarians suggest. To the extent that the Nazis have any legitimate role to play at all in the political life of this Republic—a proposition I indulge only hypothetically—the most the polity is obliged to do is respect their liberty to hold meetings, conduct discussions, and make themselves part of the public discourse. But it is not obliged to let them make use of the public streets to carry the symbols of assault and genocide to the very homes of the people who would feel most acutely and properly threatened by them.

These understandings may all arise without strain on the premises of the law as it was—the law that was built on the foundation of the *Chaplinsky* case. The question at this moment is whether those older premises will be restored. The Court still relies, as I have said, on the authority of *Chaplinsky,* but a majority has abandoned the teachings of that case, and the abandonment became manifest in 1971 with Justice Harlan's remarkable opinion in *Cohen* v. *California*. There is not enough space here to treat that case in the detail it warrants or to chart the ways in which Justice Harlan managed to overturn every premise that was essential to the doctrine in *Chaplinsky*. The case involved a young man who walked through the corridors of the County Courthouse in Los Angeles wearing a jacket that bore the inscription "Fuck the Draft." Before it was over, Harlan had sought to deploy the full moral weight of the Constitution in order to protect the "speech" on Cohen's jacket as if it were a political statement on the order of the Federalist #10. And he could not accomplish that end without revising in a radical way the traditional understanding of "speech" (let alone the concept of propriety).

In a reversal of *Chaplinsky* Harlan argued that if speech contained a residue of political significance it was presumptively protected, no matter how injurious it may be, or how void of substantive content. If the speech was presumptively protected, the burden of avoidance fell to those who felt assaulted or offended by it (and it was thought proper, in this light, to ask the victim to turn away or go elsewhere rather than ask the assailant to restrain himself in public).

But the conviction that any sign or expression was "political" depended on the reliability with which it could be said that the sign conveyed a point or stated an argument. In the case of *Cohen*, Harlan was convinced that the jacket was presenting a statement—no less—on a matter of public policy. According to Harlan, what Cohen was doing with his jacket was "asserting [a] position on the inutility or immorality of the draft." And yet it should have been apparent that "Fuck the Draft" did not necessarily mean either one of those things—that the draft was "immoral" or "inutile." Very likely it meant neither. The profanity on the jacket, like most expressions that have acquired the status of "swear words," had a certain coarseness to it that was an important part of its meaning and of the purpose for which it was used. There was no substantive argument about the military draft that Cohen would have been prevented from making if he had merely been asked to remove his jacket (and his sign) in a public place. And for the same reason, there would be no decent substantive argument that the American Nazis would be prevented from making if they were merely restrained from carrying out a provocative march into the Jewish neighborhoods of Skokie.

But Harlan's opinion in the *Cohen* case ruled out this traditional understanding because it denied at its root that there were knowable differences any longer between decent and indecent expression. "One man's vulgarity," said Harlan, "is another's lyric," and it was precisely "because governmental officials cannot make principled distinctions in this area" that the Constitution left these "matters of taste and style so largely to the individual." What Harlan denied, then, was the existence of any standards for identifying speech that was truly offensive, because the offensiveness of the words depended entirely on the subjective feelings of the people who heard them. And therefore it could only be, as he remarked, that the decision as to what language is fit for a public place must be left "largely [in] the hands of each of us."

With the full sweep of Harlan's opinion one comes to discover what it takes these days to gain a reputation for "modernity" and innovation in certain quarters of the legal profession: it requires the absorption, with an unwonted suddenness, of novel doctrines of philosophy thirty years *after* they have been discredited in the schools of philosophy. Long after the doctrines of "logical positivism" have lost their adherents in the academies, the discovery of these doctrines by Justice Harlan has been taken by many lawyers as a revolution in the law. The experience may merely remind us of the distance that has separated the schools of law from the discipline of philosophy, and it may confirm what has often been suspected: that much of what passes these days as jurisprudence is really nothing more than third-rate philosophy.

At the risk of oversimplification it may suffice here to say that the "logical positivists" were disposed to argue, with Justice Harlan, that statements which conveyed moral judgments were ultimately dependent on nothing more than subjective feelings or personal beliefs, and therefore they could not be reckoned as true or false in any strict sense. At most they were emotive statements that conveyed a sense of likes and dislikes. And so if someone condemned the use of narcotics, all one could say is that he "disliked" the use of narcotics (much in the way, as Mr. David Hamlin says, that the residents of Skokie "dislike" the Nazis). One could not prove, in this view, that it is ultimately "right" or "wrong" to use narcotics (or to "dislike" the Nazis), any more than it is right or wrong, say, to like parsley.

But as the linguists would explain, the meaning of words cannot be as subjective and arbitrary as that. Moral terms have the function of commending and condemning, approving and rejecting, and they cannot play the role they do in our language—they cannot initiate a process of reasoned discourse over moral judgments—unless the people who use these words understand, when they use them, that they are condemning or commending a course of action to others. For that to be so, the words that serve the function of commending and condemning must be established rather plainly in common usage. The meaning of words, of course, may alter over time, and many pejorative terms, like "robber" or "thief," may be uttered in jest, or in circumstances that render their meaning innocent. But at any given moment, anyone who lives with a language every day must have a fairly reliable sense of the words that are fixed very clearly in the language as terms of insult and defamation, and the expressions that may be on the borderline between derision and neutrality.

If there is any lingering disposition to believe that offensive words or verbal assaults are entirely subjective in character, one need only apply this simple test: Ten years ago Governor George Romney was running in the presidential primary in New Hampshire, and in the heat of the campaign he referred to Senator Percy of Illinois as an "opportunist." When Percy took offense Romney sought to repair the damage. He explained that, when he called Percy an "opportunist" he simply meant that Percy was an intelligent man who took advantage of his opportunities. That is to say, he was merely "describing" Percy rather than judging him, and if anything, he suggested, his remark should have been taken as a compliment: he was actually commending Percy for alertness in rising to opportunities.

The measure of one's willingness to believe, with Justice Harlan, that expressions of insult or defamation depend on nothing more than the subjective feelings of the people who hear them, is one's willingness to believe Romney's account of what he meant.

These understandings were part of the perspective that was bound up with the *Chaplinsky* case, and the question again is, Where does that case now stand in our law? Two years after Justice Harlan's opinion in *Cohen* v. *California*, the Supreme Court confirmed a wide latitude of power to local governments in the regulation of obscenity. The Court invoked the *Chaplinsky* case as the foundation for its judgment in *Paris Adult Theatre* v. *Slaton*, and, in his opinion for the majority, Chief Justice Burger made it apparent that the invocation was more than a ritualistic exercise. Burger's substantive comments on the case followed the logic of the understanding in *Chaplinsky*, and indeed he seemed intent on pressing the point that the logic of *Chaplinsky* simply could not be displaced from the law: for the benefit, apparently, of some of his colleagues, the Chief Justice observed that the " 'live' performance of a man and woman locked in a sexual embrace at high noon in Times Square [would not be] protected by the Constitution because they simultaneously engaged in a valid political dialogue." The Chief Justice surely must have known that, within the terms of Harlan's opinion in *Cohen* v. *California*, there would have been no basis on which to restrain an act of this kind.

Yet the law should be obliged to restrain this "expression," and it is Justice Murphy's opinion in *Chaplinsky* that explains, far more persuasively than anything else, the grounds on which the law may be exercised in this case. The couple could be restrained from their public gesture without interfering in any degree with their freedom to make any substantive arguments about the issues of the day. And because their sexual demonstration is not strictly necessary to "the exposition of ideas," the government might well be justified in acting out of a concern for the sensibilities of other people in a public place.

It would take a complicated argument, however, to explain just why a public display of sexual intercourse should be taken as an injury or offense to the public. The argument could be made, but it would be far more difficult than the argument that is needed to explain why Nazism is a wrong and why the presence of the Nazis in Skokie inflicts injuries. The wrongness of Nazism is of course separate from the palpable injuries that the American Nazis foster with their presence in the streets; but those injuries are clearly present.

A Supreme Court that knows why the couple may be restrained should be able to explain also why the Nazis may be restrained. The only question is whether the Court is prepared to overcome its recent distractions and admit to itself more fully that the teaching of *Chaplinsky* cannot be effaced in any society that would preserve the integrity of its public discourse and preserve itself, beyond everything else, as a decent society.

For years, the ACLU has professed to believe, with Justice Holmes, that "the best test of truth is the power of the thought to get itself accepted in the competition of the market." With all proper allowances for that curious proposition, one may still ask: What unresolved issue in the marketplace of ideas may the Nazis help to settle for us?

In the judgment of the ACLU, is there something in the perspective of the Nazis which has a plausible claim to truth? If we restrict the speech of the Nazis is it conceivable that we may shield ourselves from ideas that may turn out one day to be valid? Is it possible, for example, that a convincing case could yet be made for genocide if people were given a bit more time to develop the argument? Might it be that the commitment to a democratic regime itself stands on premises that may be shown one day to be doubtful?

These possibilities could not be ruled out if, in fact, all judgments of moral right and wrong rested on nothing more than "opinion." But the wrongness of genocide arises from the concept of morals itself, and therefore no amount of discussion, now or in the future, could possibly have any effect on its moral status. The wrongness of the act inheres in the willingness to put to death a whole group of people with no reference to criminal acts, with no discriminations to be made between the innocent and the guilty. Genocide will continue to be wrong as long as the notion of morals itself exists—as long as it is possible to speak of the difference between innocence and guilt, of the difference between killings that are justified and those that are unjustified.

In the meantime, however, the ACLU is helping to preserve the Nazis as an established part of the public arena, and the public lessons that are drawn from the experience are not apt to be wholesome. If the ACLU bends its efforts, after all, to support a *right* of the Nazis to march, what other lesson does it hope to teach but that the Nazis must be regarded as *legitimate*—that their claim to exist and speak stands on the same plane of legitimacy as that of any other group within the country. But if the Nazis are legitimate, they cannot be dismissed out of hand as implausible, and if the perspective they represent is regarded as plausible, then the self-evident "truth" on which the American regime is founded cannot in fact be a "truth." It must be merely an "opinion," no more or less likely to

be true than any other "opinion" about the nature of a
good political regime, including the "opinion" represented
by the Nazis.

But the consequence that arises from this understanding
was set forth long ago by Lincoln: If democracy were not
founded on a natural truth—on the capacity of human
beings for moral judgment—then it had to be founded
merely on "opinion": it had to arise merely because it was
the form of government that happened to be approved by
the opinions of a majority. And if the opinions of the majority were the only authoritative source of law, there could
be no ground on which one could challenge the decisions
of a majority in the name of a more fundamental law.
It would be within the competence of a majority, then, to
forgo democratic government for the entire society or to
withdraw the protections of the Constitution from any
minority. The irony is that the ACLU sees itself as defending at this moment the freedom of a minority, but the principles on which it mounts that defense would cut the
ground out from under constitutional government itself
and, in that sense, would also imperil the freedom of all
minorities.

Nearly two hundred years ago, when a current of cal-
umnies directed at Catholics was running through England,
Edmund Burke observed that "if it exists at all [in Bristol,
the city he represented], the laws have crushed its exer-
tions, and our morals have shamed its appearance in day-
light." Burke spoke here out of a tradition that regarded
the injuries inflicted through speech and expression as a
species of injustice that the law was obliged to restrain.
But he also understood the connection between the law
and the climate of opinion that could support the law and
render its strenuous exercise less necessary. As the ACLU
seeks now to resist the use of the law in restraining acts of
assault and intimidation, it is also seeking to alter in a
radical way the understanding of the public about the
foundations on which its own freedom is established. The

result of this teaching, however, is to render those foundations less firm. The measure of the difference between our age and Burke's is that the lawyers and professionals who have borne the largest responsibility for the preservation of constitutional government no longer seem to understand the moral premises on which that government rests.

THE A.C.L.U. AGAINST ITSELF [3]

Security guards stood grimly at the door of the panel on "Free Speech For Racists and Totalitarians." The discussion—at the American Civil Liberties Union's recent Convocation on Free Speech—focused on the ACLU's disputed defense of American Nazis' right to march in Skokie, Illinois. Some people feared that the Nazis themselves might show up at the panel, others expected a demonstration by the Jewish Defense League.

Among those on the dais was David Goldberger, a young ACLU lawyer who brought the action on behalf of the Nazis. Mr. Goldberger's life has been changed by that suit. He has been subjected to torrents of abuse from Jews and others horrified at the notion of defending those who unleashed the Holocaust. Some of the hostility was evident among the 300 people who crowded the Rhinelander Gallery of the New York Hilton that morning in mid-June. "This way to Auschwitz," gibed a bystander. And after Mr. Goldberger had spoken, a woman in a flowered dress rose at the back of the room to ask in a trembling voice: "Would you defend the Nazis if they wanted to march in your neighborhood?"

For a moment Mr. Goldberger remained silent. The only sound in the room was the rustling of paper and the clicking of camera shutters. Then the young lawyer replied gravely: "Lady, defending them is like having them march in my neighborhood."

[3] Article by J. Anthony Lukas, Pulitzer Prize winning journalist and author. New York *Times Magazine*. p 9-11. Jl. 9, '78 © by The New York Times Company. Reprinted by permission.

The prolonged battle over Skokie has indeed been as if the Nazis were marching through the ACLU's own neighborhood, goose-stepping across the lawns, trampling on the flower beds. The intrusion has caused great anguish, turned neighbor against neighbor, even led some people to move out. Nobody is sure just how many people have left the ACLU over Skokie. More than 4,000 have invoked the Nazis in irate letters; so thousands more, certainly, have dropped quietly off the rolls for the same reason.

But the membership decline began long before David Goldberger got his first call from the Nazis in April 1977. From a high of 270,000 in 1974, the rolls had already fallen to 210,000 by last year and have now tumbled to 185,000. Clearly, the organization's troubles stem from something much deeper than Skokie. Amid the rampant privatism of the late 70s, there is no public issue capable of generating sustained commitment from large numbers of civil libertarians. Moreover, the public-interest field, which the ACLU once had largely to itself, is now crowded with dozens of groups spawned by the 60s, all scrambling for slices of the smaller pie. Finally, this has happened at a time when America's liberal community—long the principal source of ACLU strength—is in terrible disarray. In the 60s and early 70s, liberalism was an easy reflex involving issues far from home: civil rights (in Selma and Little Rock), the war (in Saigon and Phnom Penh), Watergate and impeachment (in Washington). For Northern liberals at least, these were stark moral watersheds, dividing the good guys from the bad guys. But the liberal issues of the mid-70s are not so easy, in part because they are less remote. Affirmative action, women's rights, busing, children's rights and the like hit the liberals' own neighborhoods—even their own families—requiring painful self-examination.

Often they involve a conflict of rights: Busing, for example, wins support from libertarians determined to provide equal educational opportunity to all, but opposition from libertarians who believe parents ought to have the maximum freedom to determine how their child should be educated. Privacy pits those who want to prevent public intrusion into private lives against those who believe the press must be free to print anything except libel. The Bakke case found those committed to enlarged opportunities for blacks and other minorities opposing those who regarded racial criteria, for whatever purpose, as anathema. (The ACLU opposed Bakke, but the Supreme Court's recent decision dramatically illustrated the split in the national consciousness of such rights. Justice Powell provided the decisive vote in two 5-4 decisions: first holding that Bakke had been discriminated against because he was white, but then switching to the other side and holding that affirmative action programs were constitutional so long as race was regarded as only one of many factors.)

It is enough to make a civil libertarian yearn for the old simplicities. "Bring back Bull Connor, Richard Nixon and that gorgeous, evil war," one of the ACLU's leaders joked over a drink at the recent convocation.

Curiously, Skokie was not an issue that involved competing civil-liberties concerns. The libertarian argument was strongly on the side of the Nazis—or more accurately, against the Chicago suburb of Skokie, which passed ordinances to prevent Frank Collin and his storm troopers from marching. The ACLU's leadership regarded Skokie as a classic First Amendment case. "If we don't belong in Skokie I don't know where we belong," says Norman Dorsen, the ACLU's chairman.

Some critics of the ACLU argued that the Skokie march would not have been protected free speech at all, but incitement to riot. Yet, in the law, one can "incite" only one's own followers to riot, and nobody feared a riot by Mr. Collin's 20 stormtroopers. The real threat of disorder came from the crowds of distraught Skokie residents. To have prohibited the march on such grounds would have been to permit what is known as "the heckler's veto," lending credence to the noxious principle that speakers may be silenced because of the response expected to their words. The courts agreed with the ACLU's position, and permitted the Nazis' march, which they ultimately canceled and rescheduled for a park in Chicago.

If Skokie was an easy case in law, it was hard on the facts. For it revived the worst agony of our time. Skokie has an unusually high percentage of Holocaust survivors and no-body—certainly not the ACLU's heavily Jewish leadership—underestimates the anguish which Nazi uniforms and insignia must cause to those who lost families at Dachau and Buchenwald. One Skokie resident adamantly opposed to the Nazi march is Sol Golstein, a 64-year-old émigré from Lithuania. He recalls the Gestapo tossing his mother, starved but still alive, into a mass grave. "When men went back the next day they saw the earth move . . . I don't know what would happen to me if I saw a swastika in front of my house."

The ACLU has defended free speech for Nazis before. In 1960, for example, it represented George Lincoln Rockwell, the late American Nazi Party leader, and about 1,000 members resigned, but the incident created nothing like the Skokie stir. What has changed is not the Nazi threat—there are still barely 1,000 of them in the country—but Jewish sensibilities. In 1960, most American Jews were solid partners in the liberal coalition. Today, many see themselves as abandoned by their former allies on a host of issues—including affirmative action, black-community control, crime and Israel. Several affiliates report that many people blame the ACLU for high crime rates. In May 1977, 500 persons—many of them apparently Jewish—gathered outside its New York headquarters to protest its "protection" of criminals. "We've had enough!" shouted the crowd. When an ACLU spokeswoman told them she didn't like crime either but the rights of criminal defendants had to be protected, a demonstrator screamed, "You ought to be raped and mugged, then you'd know what we're all about."

Viewed in this context, Skokie is less cause than symbol for Jews—who until recently made up 40 percent of the ACLU's membership. One Jewish woman recently wrote that "for years I have been watching with dismay a lot of

ACLU actions and saying to myself, sooner or later they'll be defending Nazis. Now, lo and behold, here you are defending Nazis."

Another grouping disaffected over the defense of the Nazis is the ideological left. Marxists and other radicals have long been ambivalent about the organization. At the beginning—1920—the ACLU was overtly a left-wing organization, an offshoot of the American Union Against Militarism, a group of pacifists and reformers opposed to United States entry into World War I. The ACLU quickly became involved in defending the left from the notorious "Palmer Raids" and other acts of political repression. In the 1930s, it shifted toward political respectability. Spearheaded by Norman Thomas, a leader of the Socialist Party, a faction on the board moved to purge Communists from its leadership. Following the Nazi-Soviet pact, it expelled one of the ACLU's founders, Elizabeth Gurley Flynn, because she was a party member. Twenty-six years later, in April 1976, the board voted 32 to 18 to repeal Flynn's expulsion finding that it was "not consonant with the basic principles on which the ACLU was founded."

But between those dates, it did some other things that most of its current leaders admit were hardly reconcilable with its basic principles. The 1950s were a particularly bad decade for the ACLU, as they were for many American liberals. Responding to cold-war pressures, the board ordered that membership applications specify that the ACLU welcomed only those "whose devotion to civil liberties is not qualified by adherence to Communist, fascist, KKK or other totalitarian doctrine." More important, it dodged many issues in that witch-hunting era, declining to fight blacklisting and holding that the death sentence against Julius and Ethel Rosenberg raised no civil-liberties issues.

By 1951, I. F. Stone and several other civil libertarians formed the Emergency Civil Liberties Committee "to augment the ACLU, but with guts enough to fight the evils of McCarthyism without fear of being sullied by the label of 'pro-Communist.'" Only last year did it become clear just how bad things had gotten. Under the Freedom of Information Act, the ACLU obtained documents revealing that, in the 50s, five key officers of the organization maintained "questionable contacts" with the F.B.I. and that one of them served as an informer, providing the bureau with information on ACLU members. It is to the Union's credit that, when Aryeh Neier, its executive director, discovered the incriminating information, he promptly made it public along with a statement condemning the contacts as a "betrayal" of ACLU principles.

Through the 1960s and early 1970s, the Marxist left and the ACLU managed to bury their differences in the common fight against the war and Richard Nixon. But, with the disappearance of those unifying issues, their divergent perspectives have reasserted themselves. Last April 20, for example, Aryeh Neier journeyed out to the Brooklyn Law School to debate the issue with Marshall Perlin, a National Lawyers Guild member who has represented a long line of left-wing political dissidents.

It had been a tough day already for Mr. Neier. It was Hitler's birthday, the day the Nazis had originally planned to march in Skokie. And that afternoon the Jewish Defense League had staged a demonstration at ACLU headquarters, presenting the director with an extraordinary work of art— a brass plaque, engraved: "Presented to the ACLU on Hitler's Birthday. Our graves are flooded with blood and tears. Our graves are crowded with the bones of our babies and families. Where are you our brother?" the plaque affixed to a large board covered with pictures of concentration camp ovens, the whole thing covered with broken glass and simulated blood. The irony was powerful, for Mr. Neier is a German Jew and was born in Berlin on April 22, 1937. His mother told him that she had struggled to prolong her pregnancy so he would not be born on April 20 and thus have to watch stormtroopers marching through the streets to celebrate the birthday he would have shared with the Führer. The Neier family left Germany when Aryeh was two, but he lost three grandparents and several aunts, uncles and cousins in the Holocaust.

First to speak was Mr. Neier, whose moon face and chubby torso disguise a rapier intelligence and formidable debating skill: "The right to free speech is always tested at the extremes," he said. "Rarely are centrist groups denied their First Amendment rights. It is almost always fringe groups—people who are provocative, who select that place where they are disliked the most because that is where they can get the most attention. Isn't that what Martin Luther King did at Selma? For that very reason it is the extremes that have the greatest interest in protecting the rights of their enemies. Once the freedom of one group is abridged, that infringement will be cited to deny the rights of others. The people who most need the ACLU to defend the rights of the Klan are the blacks. The people who most need the ACLU to defend the rights of Nazis are the Jews."

Marshall Perlin, a big bear of a man, began with a disclaimer. "I don't wish to oppose free speech. But Mr. Neier's remarks have an abstract, neutral quality. The law is not neutral. The courts are not neutral. The ACLU is not as neutral as it pretends. The ACLU did not defend the rights of Communists in the 1950s. Why should it be defending people like the Nazis and the Klan today?"

"We were wrong in the 50s," Mr. Neier snapped. "But our failures then shouldn't be invoked as an excuse for comparable failures today. . . ."

The Mississippi case has been even more troublesome. It developed after the Harrison County Board of Education, which has been implementing a school desegregation plan, refused to let the Klan hold a rally in a school playground on a Saturday. The Grand Dragon called the ACLU's Mississippi office and the executive director accepted the case. By a narrow vote, the affiliate's board approved the decision, but all seven blacks on the board resigned in protest. When the Klan later sought to switch its suit from state to Federal court, the board reversed itself and refused to take the case, citing the Klan's record of violent acts against blacks. The Klan then asked the national ACLU to take the case and its board voted 47-15 to do so, holding to its principle that speech and assembly, as distinct from illegal action, must be protected. Bitter recriminations followed. Mississippi's representative on the national charged that Aryeh Neier told him they had to represent the Klan because Jews would never understand if they defended the Nazis in Skokie but dropped the Klan case in Mississippi under pressure from blacks.

Dramatic as the Klan cases are ultimately they posed little more legal difficulty than Skokie. For they too are relatively straight free-speech cases, and the ACLU has a long history of taking virtually any First Amendment case offered to it. First Amendment cases still have top priority, as in the ACLU's current petition that the Supreme Court review its recent decision permitting surprise police searches of newspaper offices.

The decisive dilemmas facing the organization today are in different areas. One overriding question is how far the ACLU should move from a focus on "core" civil liberties to a broader range of political and social issues. The Union has already shifted rather decisively in this direction. As late as 1960, the organization was still a relatively small (45,000 members) outfit, heavily concentrated in New York, devoted principally to filing amicus curiae briefs in free-speech and due-process cases. In 1964, Charles Morgan Jr. opened a Southern regional office in Atlanta and largely through the force of his iconoclastic personality dragged what was by then the rather elitist organization into the battle to secure the rights of black people. Henceforth, rights of "equality" —those embodied in the Thirteenth, Fourteenth and Fifteenth Amendments and hitherto pigeonholed as "civil rights" rather than "civil liberties"—commanded an increasingly important place on the ACLU agenda.

If civil rights woke the organization out of its cold-war lethargy, the Vietnam war plunged it directly into the social activism of the 60s. One turning point was the Spock trial of 1968. When Dr. Benjamin Spock and four co-defendants were indicted in Boston for counseling draft evasion, the national board initially declined to take the case because it feared it would raise "non-civil liberties issues," such as the legality of the war. But, after the Massachusetts affiliate took the case, the board reversed itself in a wrenching decision that led to a batch of resignations.

Behind the opening wedge of the Spock case, the group pushed ever more deeply into the war issue, defending many draft resisters and military dissidents. By July 1970, following the Cambodian invasion and Kent State, it had traveled so far that it could pass a resolution calling for the "immediate termination" of the war.

Watergate and impeachment took the ACLU even further into matters which some of its members still regarded as "political." In September 1973, after some bitter wrangling and a 51-5 vote, it became the first major national organization to call for Mr. Nixon's impeachment. It followed with a series of full-page ads in major papers appealing for funds to pursue the matter. The ads were launched with great trepidation—some officers feared a disaster—but they were a staggering success, helping attract a record 50,000 new members in 1973 alone.

Again it was Chuck Morgan, from his new base in Washington, who led the impeachment charge, brandishing his flaming sword. This made some board members nervous, among them Edward J. Ennis, then the ACLU's chairman, who wrote several memos urging circumspection. The strains surfaced at an executive-committee meeting when Mr. Ennis and other members joined in criticizing Mr. Morgan's zeal. The Washington director felt that Aryeh Neier did not adequately support him—and this set off a bitter feud.

"You have to understand Chuck's experience in the South to see why he was so angry at Aryeh," one staffer recalls. "When you are battling the Klan and the White Citi-

zens Council down there you expect perfidy from your enemies, but you also demand absolute loyalty from your
friends. He felt betrayed by Aryeh."

Mr. Neier, on the other hand, is not a man who permits
himself much public emotion. Most members of the organization regard him as one of the brightest people they have
ever met, but he is pure, undiluted cerebrum. His prodigi-
ous intellectuality is relieved only occasionally by chess
and J. S. Bach. One staffer recalls an impromptu celebra-
tion in her office the day the Vietnam war ended. Mr. Neier
looked through the door and remarked coolly, "I don't see
this as a victory. There's no First Amendment in North
Vietnam."

One man who knows him well says, "Aryeh's substance
is left, but his style is right. He was elected in 1970 as the
candidate of the left and in the early years, often in close
working partnership with Chuck Morgan, he was responsible for pushing the organization into some of its boldest
positions. But increasingly he came to feel more at home
personally with the cool traditionalists on the board, least
at home with the passionate progressives. And when Aryeh
doesn't respect you intellectually, you cease to exist for
him."

For a time it was a shoot-out in the libertarian corral
and, ultimately, the cool marksman from New York got his
man. When Mr. Neier chastised him in 1976 for speaking
out on the presidential campaign without sufficiently sepa-
rating his position from the ACLU's, Mr. Morgan took high
umbrage and chose that as the occasion on which to resign
as Washington director. (About the same time, Melvin L.
Wulf, the ACLU's legal director, resigned after differences
with Mr. Neier and Mr. Dorsen.)

The turmoil of recent years—including the membership
decline, management imbroglios, Skokie and the battles
with Mr. Morgan, Mr. Wulf and the board's left wing—
took their toll on Aryeh Neier. Last year, he decided that
he wanted to leave within a year. Chairman Dorsen, a New
York University law professor with a magic touch for heal-

ing organizational wounds, urged him to stay on a while so it would not appear that he was resigning under fire on Skokie. Mr. Neier's own pride was justifiably involved, as a friend explains: "Aryeh's like a baseball star who had some big .350 seasons, but has just come off a couple of disastrous .230 ones. He wants to go out with at least a .300 season under his belt." Finally, in April, he announced his intention to leave in early fall.

A committee has been formed to seek a successor. As of this writing, the two principal candidates from within the organization are Ira Glasser, the volatile, earthy executive director of the New York affiliate, and board member Monroe H. Freedman, a cool but quirky gadfly who is professor of law at Hofstra. The two men are often seen as representing competing wings—Mr. Freedman, the traditionalists, and Mr. Glasser, the progressives—though they themselves maintain they are closer on most issues than is generally recognized. Both men agree that the essential task before the organization is to apply eighteenth- and nineteenth-century libertarian principles to twentieth-century settings. They also agree that it must be rigorous in establishing genuine civil-liberties issues in the new areas rather than merely seeking plausible rationales for essentially political activity. The principal difference between the two men is temperamental; on his record, Mr. Glasser would be somewhat more eager than Mr. Freedman to find suitable grounds for extending the ACLU's reach.

The debate over such extension is complicated by the apparent lessons of recent years. Most ACLU leaders now recognize that its vast growth between 1965 and 1975 was somewhat artificial, built on people who were less interested in civil liberties than in fighting the war on Mr. Nixon. It is widely believed that most of those who quit over Skokie were people who were never committed to, perhaps never even understood, the First Amendment. The dilemma is a complex one. In the palmy days of the Warren Court, the ACLU did not need a large membership or a full treasury to win battles; it merely filed a brief before a generally sympathetic court. But with the Burger Court hostile to many of its concerns, the emphasis has shifted to lobbying and public education. "To win these days," says John F. Shattuck, the new Washington director, "we need clout out there in the country."

On the other hand, there is intense awareness that the ACLU can never aspire to anything like majority support: By definition, civil liberties are rights against the majority. The need is to maintain if not a majority then at least a substantial constituency for what are often called the "core" rights—particularly the First Amendment rights of speech and assembly without which no other rights can be assured. But as the organization seeks to widen its constituency by expanding into other areas, there is concern as to whether the conflicts engendered will erode the constituency for the "core" rights. For example, Catholics who might rally around the First Amendment are alienated by the ACLU stance on abortion; and Jews were put off by its opposition to Allan Bakke. "I'm not worried about alienating people; we wouldn't be doing our job unless we did," says Rolland O'Hare, one of the traditionalists on the board. "But I do get worried when we start making it difficult to defend the things we care most about."

The argument is carried furthest by Alan Dershowitz, a professor of law at Harvard and a former board member, who feels the ACLU shouldn't be trying to develop new constituencies. "The Union should be like an accordion," he says. "In some decades it should expand, in others it should contract. The ACLU is merely a limited insurance policy against specific types of repression. When that repression isn't there, we shouldn't try to expand to fill the vacuum."

Some critics accused the ACLU of doing just that. They point to a speech Mr. Neier gave at a conference in 1976 in which he noted that in the postwar-and-Watergate doldrums the only segment of 60s activists still able to generate widespread excitement was the movement for women's rights. Somewhat later, Mr. Neier described the organization as "the legal branch of the women's movement." Indeed, under vigorous prodding from the "women's caucus" in the organization—women's issues have gained an increasingly important place on the agenda. In October 1977, the board voted to designate as its "No. 1 priority" the campaign to guarantee women the right to choose an abortion. "Do we really feel that's the No. 1 civil-liberties issue in the country," a skeptical board member asks, "or are we trying to tap into the vitality of the women's movement?"

A number of areas into which the ACLU has expanded aggressively during Mr. Neier's tenure have aroused relatively little controversy within the organization. One is the effort to guarantee constitutional rights to people confined in institutions—jails, prisons, mental hospitals, training schools for children and nursing homes for the elderly—settings in which until recently rights were regarded as barely applicable and virtually unenforceable.

There are other issues that still sharply divide the board. A recent question that developed considerable heat was whether the ACLU should support a suit by an Idaho factory seeking an injunction against inspections by the Occupational Safety and Health Administration without a warrant. Originally, the board voted to side with the company, holding that the Fourth Amendment prohibition against unreasonable searches applied to safety checks on corporations, but, then, by a 30-20 vote, it reversed itself. Ultimately, the Supreme Court ruled in favor of the company.

The most divisive issue of all these days is a perennial debate about whether the ACLU should get into what is called "economic rights." The left on the board has long argued that people cannot exercise their constitutional rights without an adequate income. "Rosa Parks [the originator of the Montgomery bus boycott] couldn't have gotten on that bus without a nickel," says Ellen Feingold, a leader of the fight. At a recent meeting, another board member thundered: "By our silence we would be defending the status quo." Opponents argue that such arguments seek to "equate civil liberties and social justice, while they are very different things."

At last December's meeting, the board passed, 37-30, a relatively mild resolution which held that "when there is a direct and substantial connection between poverty and particular deprivations of civil liberties and civil rights, the ACLU will support positive governmental action to mitigate the effects of poverty." But it voted down, 29-16, a much more far-reaching resolution declaring that "the right of gainful employment ought to be recognized as the fundamental right of every American."

Much of the board believes the most pressing matter facing the organization is not economic rights for the poor but the ACLU's own economic survival. The long-term membership slide, and its severe impact on revenue, forced cutbacks in program and staff. Management consultants concluded this spring that the organization was in "deep financial trouble." They traced the trouble less to its involvement in controversial issues like Skokie than to what they call "systemic weakness." In particular, they blamed disastrous management of the membership department, inadequate record-keeping and poor communications with members. Those familiar with the situation say the ACLU did not adapt quickly enough to the transition from the easy impeachment days when, according to an office joke, you could send out a letter reading, "Dear Sir, Screw You," and get back $20. Such bland self-assurance probably led Mr. Neier and others to ignore membership details. (Membership dues support all the organization's First Amendment activities. Some critics of the Skokie defense argue that the Nazis had enough money to engage their own lawyers, and an organization that depends so heavily on Jewish money shouldn't be paying to represent a group that wanted to kill Jews. To which an ACLU official responds: "We have never had a means test here. The New York *Times* has plenty of money, too, but if they want our defense on something like the Pentagon Papers, we would be glad to defend them.")

Of late, Mr. Neier has poured much of his personal

energy into raising money from foundations. Indeed, the management consultants give him credit for a "superb job" in raising $2 million in such grants. However, these monies are designated for specific projects, like those on women's rights, privacy and censorship. Some critics worry that the increasing reliance on earmarked grants permits others to set too much of the ACLU's agenda.

Mr. Neier's hope of going out with a .300 season depends largely on the success of a special fund-raising appeal, signed by David Goldberger, which has already raised some $500,-000; and on the Free Speech convocation, which drew 1,700 people and, with corporate underwriting, may raise another $250,000. The convocation also served to rally the organization's spirits, badly dampened by the recent turmoil, particularly Skokie.

Bruce J. Ennis, the ACLU's new legal director, sees Skokie as "a good thing, because it weeded out the people who don't really believe in civil liberties." Jules Feiffer, a speaker at the convocation luncheon, said much the same thing in his own oblique style. Skokie, he said, raised several questions: "Why can't we come up with a better class of victims? Whatever became of victims like Eugene Debs? Mythic victims. Victims you could hang around with. Who would enhance your status."

But there are still some ACLU members who believe in standing up for any victim who is denied his constitutional rights. One is the man from Miami who responded to the Goldberger appeal with a check and three words:

"Defend the bastards."

POSTMORTEM ON THE NAZIS [4]

At a recent panel discussion on the Nazi rally in Chicago, several points of interest emerged:

[4] Article by William F. Buckley Jr., editor, author, and magazine publisher. *National Review.* 29:1040. O. 15, '77. By permission of *National Review*, 150 E. 35th St., New York, NY 10016.

1. As a result of the sustained publicity given to the Nazis, did one have the opportunity to test their latent appeal? Certainly no one who hadn't known there was such a thing as a Nazi "movement" in America now knew it. Did the "$10 million of free publicity"—one always hears such figures mentioned, though it is hard to know if they have scientific meaning—substantially increase the rolls of the American National Socialist Party? The answer is no. However, this datum is insufficient proof that there is no latent sympathy in America for Nazi doctrines. The reason is that the kind of publicity achieved by the demonstrators was hardly evangelistic. Out of every thousand inches of copy devoted to the episode, probably not one relayed their noxious message. All one got on television, or in the press, was the placards postulating the racial superiority of the Aryans: pure slogans.

Now this is in sharp contrast with the exposure given a dozen years ago by *Playboy* magazine to the original American Nazi, George Lincoln Rockwell. Over a stretch of ten thousand words (parenthetically, the interviewer was Alex Haley, subsequently the author of *Roots*), Rockwell spun out his half-truths in monstrously plausible form. There were those (myself among them) who protested that kind of exposure given to the Nazi message. But a demonstration featuring merely the head of the boil isn't an effective instrument of proselytization: suggesting,

2. That the move to bar the demonstration was wrong-headed? The answer is in two parts. Pragmatically, it was. That is to say, the Nazi demonstration did very little harm. It did not make converts, and therefore did not bring the country a step closer to the point where advocates of interference only when there is clear and present danger would have had their day. The theoretical point however is not here accosted. Many of those who were willing to let the Nazis demonstrate were unwilling to concede the right of the government to forbid the demonstration. The most telling argument against the right of the demonstrators is that

the United States bases its Constitution on the idea of a free society. What it is that constitutes a free society is susceptible to debate, but only within limits.

There is also a debate as to where those limits lie. But there shouldn't be a debate that they lie *somewhere*. And if they lie anywhere, they lie on the safe side of the proposition that all Jews should be incinerated. Professor Walter Berns in his superb book on the First Amendment makes the point that the notion that all ideas have a right to compete in the intellectual marketplace presupposes that any one idea has the right to win. Therefore if the Nazis have the right to argue, they have the right to assume power.

But if they do assume power, intolerable results follow. These results contradict the bases of the Declaration of Independence, namely that there are "self-evident" truths. If there is one self-evident truth, it is surely that genocide cannot be tolerated. Under the circumstances, the toleration of the Nazis' demonstration was exactly that—an indulgence, not a recognition of a constitutional right. Leaving unanswered the question:

3. Was there a cogent case against even the pragmatic toleration of the demonstration? The most succinct argument in support of such a thesis was made by columnist Garry Wills. He insisted that the relevant body of law "is not the First Amendment but the nuisance statutes. The Nazis are not engaged in the rational airing of views, but in the provoking of irrational (but predictable) responses. They are, in effect, broadcasting an obscene phone call to a whole neighborhood instead of a single house."

The reasoning is persuasive. Though I am afraid to make a telephone call to establish that it is so, I assume that even the ACLU backs laws against individuals dialing a telephone number for the purpose of uttering random obscenities. This is among other things a violation of privacy. The march through Harlem by the KKK, or through Skokie by the Nazis, isn't the exercise of the right of assembly, but an obscene phone call acting as an impostor under the umbrella of the First Amendment. The final—unanswered—question is:

4. Isn't it so that when an intolerable political movement reaches the point where it constitutes a clear and present danger, it reaches also the point where as a practical matter it is impossible to stop it? Imagine trying to outlaw the Nazis in 1932. Or the Peronistas in 1945. Or, for that matter, the French, Italian, or Spanish Communists now. Against the consideration that pragmatic experience suggests we indulge the little tyrants, there is that other consideration that little tyrants sometimes—overnight—become big tyrants. The moral is that little boys should not be given dangerous toys.

FOR ALL OR FOR NONE [5]

As often happens when fundamental liberties are at stake, the principle involved in the Skokie, Illinois, right-to-march case must be isolated from the motives of the American Nazi Party, whose civil rights are here in question. The provocative facts of the "Nazis'" attempt to march in their Hitlerian get-ups through a town with a large Jewish population, many of them survivors of German totalitarianism and its death camps, are extraordinarily repellent. This handful of lunatic demonstrators (who do not pretend to have any politics, not even that of the National Socialists they claim to ape), deliberately chose to try to route their march through a town where it would cause the maximum of pain—and therefore of publicity, which is all they are really after.

Quite naturally, the authorities of this town of 70,000 on the outskirts of Chicago took strong measures to try to prevent the ugly event from taking place. They got a

[5] Article entitled "For All or For None; Right to March Case of the American Nazi Party in Skokie, Ill." Nation. 225:354–5. O. 15, '77. Reprinted by permission of the Nation Associates.

court order to bar the parade. Then they passed three ordinances aimed at preventing this kind of thing—by requiring a large insurance bond to pay for damages that might occur from incited violence, by banning parades in paramilitary uniforms and by forbidding the display of symbols, slogans or literature that libeled a group.

Clearly, these restrictions were on, if not over, the edge of constitutional protections for free speech and assembly. The "Nazis" are happy to obey the ban on the provocation they sought and to sit back and watch the case make its way up through the American judicial system, probably all the way to the top. Enter the American Civil Liberties Union.

Should it have done so? A small but significant proportion of the ACLU's members, especially in Illinois, has resigned, angrily protesting that the organization has no business defending the right to "speak" (which the law says must include the right to demonstrate) of this loathsome little group. Those former members have attractive and even plausible arguments on their side, but in our opinion their views should not prevail. All sorts of values have been called "indivisible," but freedom of speech, that most basic of liberties, is truly the one that cannot be split without starting to disappear.

So we believe that the ACLU did the right thing when it challenged in court Skokie's restrictive ordinances. Provocative demonstrations that arouse the anger of the majority are, of course, not new in this country. The Selma, Alabama march led by Martin Luther King Jr. is one famous example from the recent past. That confrontation of a minority insisting on its rights with a majority whose institutions resisted their exercise was a turning point in the long struggle for full freedom for black Americans. The Selma march would never have taken place if the authorities had been allowed to ban it on the ground that it would provoke the rage of white opponents of civil rights for black citizens and therefore endanger the peace. Police exist to keep the peace, and in fact they did so, however reluctantly, at the bridge in Selma.

Two other major arguments are used against the right of the "Nazis" to march in Skokie. One is the familiar one that nobody has a right to shout "Fire!" in a crowded theater, creating panic. But in the Skokie case, the element of "clear and present danger" inherent in that doctrine is missing. There will be plenty of time and opportunity for the people of Skokie to reply to the insults of the marchers, and thus there is no reason for panic.

The other argument is that group defamation should not be permitted. If that notion prevailed, much of literature, ancient and modern, would have to be banned—consider Shakespeare on the French. And Aryeh Neier, executive director of the ACLU, in a letter responding to protests from his membership on the Skokie matter, cites a passage in a speech at Hebrew University in Jerusalem in 1962 by the late American legal philosopher Edmond Cahn, in which he said that, if there were prohibitions against group defamation, "officials could begin by prosecuting anyone who distributed the Christian Gospels, because they contain many defamatory statements not only about the Jews but also about Christians; they show Christians failing Jesus in his hour of deepest tragedy."

In Illinois, among other places, the ACLU has a long record of defending the rights of unpopular marchers. In 1966 it was Martin Luther King Jr. in Cicero. In 1968 it was the anti-war demonstrators at the Democratic Convention in Chicago (where Mayor Daley's police deliberately failed to keep the peace). Two landmark First Amendment cases (*Terminiello* and *Gregory*), reinforcing protesters' rights and therefore those of the rest of us, were handled by the Illinois branch of the ACLU. At this moment it is representing in court the Martin Luther King Coalition's right to march in Chicago's Marquette Park area. The record is impeccable because it stands on the principle that constitutional rights must be defended for all who would exercise them, not just those whom we would selectively tolerate.

Revolting as the "Nazi" contingent is, and painful as their proposed march will be to citizens who should not be afflicted by it, there is no way it can be prevented without doing serious damage to the liberties of all Americans, including the people of Skokie.

BIBLIOGRAPHY

An asterisk (*) preceding a reference indicates that the article or part of it has been reprinted in this book.

Books and Pamphlets

Berns, Walter. The First Amendment and the future of American democracy. Basic Books. '76.

Chenery, William. Freedom of the press. Greenwood Press. '78.

Clark, Todd and Novelli, Rebecca. Fair trial/free press. Benziger, Bruce & Glencoe. '77.

Corwin, Edward S. The Constitution and what it means today. Revised by Harold W. Chase and Craig R. Ducat. Princeton University Press. '78.

Dennis, Everette and others, eds. Justice Hugo Black and the First Amendment. Iowa State University Press. '78.

Dhavan, Rajeev and Davies, Christie, eds. Censorship and obscenity. Rowman & Littlefield. '78.

Franklin, Marc and Franklin, Ruth. The First Amendment and the Fourth Estate; communications law for undergraduates. Foundation Press. '77.

Fretz, Donald. Courts and the news media. National College of the State Judiciary, University of Nevada. '77.

Gallagher, Neil. How to stop the porno plague; a simple, straightforward action plan that can work in your community. Bethany Fellowship. '77.

Harris, Brian. The courts, the press and the public. Barry Rose. '76.

Hohenberg, John. A crisis for the American press. Columbia University Press. '78.

Paul, James and Schwartz, Murray. Federal censorship; obscenity in the mail. Greenwood Press. '77.

Schudson, Michael. Discovering the news: a social history of American newspapers. Basic Books. '78.

Swain, Bruce. Reporters' ethics. Iowa State University Press. '78.

Periodicals

America. 138:377. My. 13, '78. Television's day in court: NBC sued for negligence in airing Born Innocent.

America. 138:476-7. Je. 17, '78. Searching for evidence; right of law-enforcement agents to search newspaper offices; Supreme Court decision.

*America. 139:44-5. Jl. 29, '78. The "filthy words" decision.

American Scholar. 46:165-80. Spring '77. Freedom of expression: too much of a good thing? John Sparrow.

Atlantic Monthly. 239:29-34. F. '77. Danger: pendulum swinging: using the courts to muzzle the press. Alan Schwartz.

*Atlantic Monthly. 239:37-41. My. '77. "Obscenity—forget it." Charles Rembar.

Business Week. p 27-8. My. 15, '78. Right-to-speak ruling business may regret.

Center Magazine. 11:17-22. Mr./Ap. '78. Rating the media. Hugh Downs.

*Center Magazine. 11:8-16. Jl./Ag. '78. A secretive security; national security and the First Amendment; questions and answers. David Wise.

*Christian Century. 94:451-3. My. 11, '77. Letting go: everybody has the right to be wrong. Jean Lyles.

Christianity and Crisis. 38:21. F. 20, '78. High noon in Skokie. Arthur Moore.

Columbia Journalism Review. 17:43-50. N./D. '78. The press and the courts: Is news gathering shielded by the First Amendment?

Crawdaddy, p 60. My. '78. Gag order's no joke for defendants. William Kunstler.

Current. p 32-8. F. '77. Coming of bold pornography; interviews ed. by Walter Goodman. Ernest van den Haag; Gay Talese.

Current. p 3-7. Jl./Ag. '78. Press and privacy. Arthur Miller.

Current Biography. 39:22-5. N. '78. Aryeh Neier.

Editorial Research Reports. v 2, no 24:983-6. D. 23, '77. Media reformers. William Thomas.

English Journal. 66:12-25. F. '77. Censorship, the law, and the teacher of English; symposium. Allan Glatthorn.

English Journal. 66:18-20. F. '77. Censorship and the schools: a different perspective; studying community standards of obscenity in Jefferson County, Ky. Stanley Mour.

Forbes. 122:85. S. 18, '78. Losing battle; defending pornography. James Cook.

Good Housekeeping. 184:103+. Mr. '77. Dirty movies! Dirty books! ideas of L. Parrish. Charles Remsberg and Bonnie Remsberg.

Harper's. 254:12+. Ap. '77. Confusion worse confounded. Lewis Lapham.

Intellect. 106:99-100. S. '77. Current status of obscenity laws. Frederick Schauer.

Journal of Criminal Law & Criminology. 68:583-90. D. '77. First Amendment—free speech.

Journal of Criminal Law & Criminology. 68:613-23. D. '77. First Amendment—obscenity.

Journalism Quarterly. 54:690-6. Winter '77. Private property vs. reporter rights—a problem in news gathering. John Watkins.

Legal Briefs for Editors, Publishers, and Writers. v 2, no 10:1, 6-7. O. '78. Furor continues over Farber.

Library Journal. 102:1543, 1573-80. Ag. '77. Debate nobody won; The Speaker; criticism of the film, with editorial comment. John Berry.

Discussion. Library Journal. 102:2289-90. N. 15, '77.

Maclean's. 91:49-50. Jl. 24, '78. Six-and-a-half years to 1984—and counting. Michael Posner.

Mademoiselle. 83:94. My. '77. Intelligent woman's guide to sex; L. Flynt's obscenity trial. Karen Durbin.

Ms. 6:22. Ap. '78. Teenager's poem on trial. Terry Kennedy.

Nation. 224:99-100. Ja. 29, '77. First Amendment hustle; trial of Hustler magazine publishers.

Nation. 225:110-13. Ag. 6-13, '77. Judicial thicket: the Supreme Court and obscenity. Mel Friedman.

*Nation. 225:354-5. O. 15, '77. For all or none; right to march case of the American Nazi Party in Skokie, Ill.

Nation. 226:82-4. Ja. 28, '78. Right to make waves: free press in the high schools; new California law. Mike Wiener.

*Nation. 226:105-8. F. 4, '78. Obscenity and the law: the way the wind blows. Peter Michelson.

*Nation. 226:422-8. Ap. 15, '78. Right to be offensive: Skokie—the extreme test; National Socialist Party. Carl Cohen.

Reply with rejoinder. Nation. 226:522+. My. 6, '78. Gilbert Gordon.

Nation. 226:589-90. My. 20, '78. You and I and corporate management: decision in First National Bank of Boston v. Bellotti. Melvin Wulf.

Nation. 226:748. Je. 24, '78. Snooping about in the files; Supreme Court decision allowing police to enter news offices without warning.

Nation. 226:757-61. Je. 24, '78. Genocide and the Nazis; the case against group libel; defending the right of Nazis to march in Skokie, Ill. Carl Cohen.

Nation. 227:41-3. Jl. 8-15, '78. Press vs. the bench: closure is worse than a gag. David Rudenstine.

Nation. 227:146-8. Ag. 19-26, '78. Skokie's lessons on liberty. Philip Green.

Reply: Nation. 227:258+. S. 23, '78. Carl Cohen.

Nation. 227:228-9. S. 16, '78. Rights of Farber's sources. Aryeh Neier.

National Review. 29:252. Mr. 4, '77. Hustler and freedom.

*National Review. 29:712-13. Je. 24, '77. I say lock 'em up, spank them, and send them home. M. J. Sobran Jr.

*National Review. 29:1040. O. 15, '77. Postmortem on the Nazis. Wm. F. Buckley Jr.

*National Review. 29:1349-50. N. 25, '77. First Amendment pixillation.

*National Review. 30:588-93. My. 12, '78. Marching through Skokie. Hadley Arkes.

National Review. 30:641. My. 26, '78. One writer's testimony; excerpts from address. John Updike.

National Review. 30:817-18. Jl. 7, '78. Established press; Supreme Court decisions concerning the press.

National Review. 30:901-2+. Jl. 21, '78. Censorship, stereotypes, and other fine things. M. J. Sobran Jr.

Nation's Business. 65:9-10. Ap. '77. When freedom is difficult to live with. James Kilpatrick.

New Republic. 178:16-17. Ja. 28, '78. Feeding the press; Congressional press secretaries. Emily Yoffe.

New Republic. 178:5-6+. Ap. 22, '78. Springtime for Skokie; proposed march by the American Nazi party.

New York. 11:10-11. Je. 19, '78. How the Supreme Court zaps the press; search and seizure decision. Sidney Zion.

*New York Review of Books. p 36-8. O. 26, '78. The rights of Myron Farber. Ronald Dworkin.

*New York Times. p IV, 11:1. My. 7, '78. Two theories of press freedom are parallel, yet bound to meet. Floyd Abrams.

*New York Times. p A10. Jl. 28, '78. Courts and the process of news gathering. Deirdre Carmody.

*New York Times. p A17. Ag. 17, '78. The Farber case. Anthony Lewis.

*New York Times. Editorial. p A26. N. 9, '78. The doctor and the press.

New York Times. p A17. N. 16, '78. Michigan high court won't bar scrutiny of a reporter's notes.

New York Times (Letter to the Editor). p A26. N. 16, '78. "Seven dirty words" and the Court. Abbott Washburn.

New York Times. p 38. N. 19, '78. Subpoenas of notes of reporters grow. Deirdre Carmody.

New York Times Book Review. 83:31. Jl. 16, '78. Iranian visitor; book censorship. Richard Lingeman.

New York Times Magazine. p 16-17+. Mr. 6, '77. United States versus the princes of porn. Ted Morgan.

New York Times Magazine. p 18. Mr. 6, '77. Has the First Amendment met its match? Richard Neville.

*New York Times Magazine. p 11-13. Ag. 21, '77. The press, privacy and the Constitution. Floyd Abrams.
  Same with title: What of the privacy explosion? *Current History.* 196:7–17. O. '77.
  Discussions: New York *Times Magazine.* p 26+. S. 18, '77.
*New York Times Magazine. p 9-11. Jl. 9, '78. The A.C.L.U. against itself. J. Anthony Lukas.
New Yorker. 54:21. My. 29, '78. Notes and comment.
*New Yorker. 54:23. Ag. 14, '78. Notes and comment.
Newsweek. 89:34. F. 21, '77. Dirty book goes to jail; Hustler publisher L. Flynt. Peter Bonventre and others.
Newsweek. 89:13. F. 28, '77. Justice for Hustler. Arthur Kretchmer.
Newsweek. 89:66. My. 9, '77. Supreme embarrassment; news leak describing Supreme Court action on appeals in the Watergate cover-up trial. Jerrold Footlick and Lucy Howard.
*Newsweek. 90:53. N. 7, '77. Obscenity: who's to say? Kansas trial of A. Goldstein and J. Buckley. Richard Boeth and Elaine Sciolino.
Newsweek. 91:105-6. Je. 12, '78. Searching the press; police searches of news organizations; Supreme Court decision. Jerrold Footlick and Lucy Howard.
Newsweek. 91:93-4. Je. 26, '78. Court and the press. David Alpern and Diane Camper.
Newsweek. 92:41-2. Ag. 14, '78. TV on trial again; suit against NBC over airing of Born Innocent. Tony Schwartz and others.
Newsweek. 92:78. O. 2, '78. Farber loses again.
*Philadelphia Inquirer. p 9A. Ag. 17, '78. The Farber case is not a black and white issue. Bernard Borish.
Politics Today. 5:29. My./Je. '78. Courting obscenity.
Progressive. 41:6-7. D. '77. Even for Nazis; Skokie, Ill. right-to-march controversy.
  Reply: Progressive 42:60. Ap. '78. Virgil Clift.
Publishers Weekly. 211:41-2. Mr. 14, '77. Obscenity: new High Court ruling, AAP on Flynt. Susan Wagner.
Publishers Weekly. 211:42. Je. 6, '77. High court upholds criminal conviction of Smith for intrastate mailing. Susan Wagner.
Publishers Weekly. 212:29+. Jl. 25, '77. AAP cautions Senate on pending obscenity law. Susan Wagner.
Publishers Weekly. 121:16+. N. 14, '77. Washington takes three actions on obscenity issues. Susan Wagner.
Publishers Weekly. 212:23-4. D. 12, '77. St. Martin's wins round against New York obscenity law; case of Show Me! Madalynne Reuter.
Publishers Weekly. 213:58. F. 13, '78. Right-of-center censorship increasing, ALA finds. Susan Wagner.

Publishers Weekly. 213:26+. Mr. 13, '78. AAP scores obscenity laws in House testimony. Susan Wagner.

Publishers Weekly. 213:32+. My. 15, '78. Six book groups challenge new Tennessee obscenity law. Madalynne Reuter.

Publishers Weekly. 213:17. Je. 5, '78. Court removes children from obscenity definition. Susan Wagner.

Publishers Weekly. 214:81-2. Jl. 17, '78. New Tennessee obscenity law unconstitutional, court finds. Madalynne Reuter.

Publishers Weekly. 214:14. Ag. 21, '78. New York State booksellers face proposed indecency bill. Madalynne Reuter.

Publisher's Weekly. p 285. Ag. 28, '78. Farber offers draft of book to judge in Jascalevich trial.

Rolling Stone. p 17. S. 7, '78. Dollars for decency; George Carlin's recording, Filthy Words.

Saturday Review. 5:4. N: 12, '77. Fairness doctrine for the press? Norman Cousins.

*Saturday Review. 5:22-3+. Mr. 4, '78. Our all-too-timid press; excerpt from On Press. Tom Wicker.

*Saturday Review. 5:19-23. S. 16, '78. Television's trying times; Niemi v. NBC and Chronicle Publishing suit. Karl Meyer.

School Library Journal. 24:64. O. '77. Publishers and librarians protest child porn provision in New York law.

Society. 15:11+. N./D. '77. Free press for a free people; excerpt from address, March 28, 1977. Eric Sevareid.

Time. 109:51-2. F. 21, '77. Bad case makes worse law; trial of Hustler publisher, L. Flynt.

Time. 109:80. Mr. 14, '77. Editors telling secrets. Thomas Griffith.

Time. 110:40. Ag. 15, '77. First Amendment blues.

Time. 111:68. My. 8, '78. Burger's blast; right of corporations to speak out on governmental issues; Supreme Court decision.

Time. 111:68+. My. 8, '78. Rape replay; Niemi: negligence suit against NBC and the Chronicle Publishing Co.

Time. 111:101. Je. 12, '78. Right to rummage? right of police to search newsrooms; Supreme Court decision.

Time. 112:73. Jl. 10, '78. Keep out; question of press access to public facilities; Supreme Court decision.

Time. 112:85. Ag. 21, '78. TV wins a crucial case; dismissal of suit blaming NBC for a rape.

Times Literary Supplement. No 3961:233. F. 24, '78. Limits of free speech [review article]. Geoffrey Marshall.

UNESCO Courier. 30:28-31. Ap. '77. Mass media and society: American viewpoint. William Harley.

USA Today. 107:13-14. Ag. '78. Broadcasters not interested in First Amendment rights. Nicholas Johnson.

U.S. Catholic. 43:36-8. My. '78. Why the press can't report on morality. Wesley Pipert.

U.S. News & World Report. 83:34. O. 31, '77. Do we have rights to everything? John Houston.

U.S. News & World Report. 84:91. My. 8, '78. More leeway for companies to sway public.

U.S. News & World Report. 84:40. Je. 12, '78. Anti-press backlash in courts?

Vital Speeches of the Day. 43:280-3. F. 15, '77. Censorship and man's right to know; radio news; address, December 17, 1976. Kenneth Giddens.

Vital Speeches of the Day. 44:24-8. O. 15, '77. Day the First Amendment died; address, September 16, 1977. John Bittner.

Vital Speeches of the Day. 44:588-92. Jl. 15, '78. Freedom of the press; address, May 17, 1978. John Oakes.

Wall Street Journal. p 12. Ag. 23, '78. A judicial war on the press? Jonathan Kwitny.

Wall Street Journal. OpEd. O. 9, '78. Testing New Jersey's Shield Law.

Wall Street Journal. p 24. O. 24, '78. Of privacy and the press. Arthur Schlesinger Jr.

*Washington Post. p A3. Ag. 16, '78. Farber case dulls the edge of the press' silver sword. Haynes Johnson.

Washington Post. p A1. Ag. 31, '78. Court orders Farber freed, sets a hearing. Lee Lescaze.

Washington Post. p A2. S. 6, '78. New Jersey court hears arguments in press case. Lee Lescaze.

Washington Post. p B7. S. 12, '78. Snepp seeks permission to publish two articles. Jane Seaberry.

Washington Post. p A1. O. 25, '78. Doctor acquitted in murder case involving free press, fair trial. Lee Lescaze.

Washington Post. p A23. N. 3, '78. Supreme Court on the air? Charles Seib.

Wilson Library Bulletin. 51:466-7. F. '77. Another round in the obscenity battle; case of J. L. Smith. W. D. Nelson.

Wilson Library Bulletin. 51:794-5. Je. '77. ALA Exec Board delays distribution of film, The Speaker. W. R. Eshelman.